The *Cobbler's*
Left Thumb

JAMES DIKIN

PAGE PUBLISHING, INC.
Conneaut Lake, PA

First originally published by Page Publishing 2020

ISBN 978-1-64628-199-2 (pbk)
ISBN 978-1-64628-200-5 (digital)

Printed in the United States of America

To my wife, Dena, and our family.
But most of all, to my Lord and Savior, Jesus Christ.

Contents

Acknowledgement

I want to especially thank my wife, Jeanie, and our kids—Bob, Connie, and Wendy—for their patience while I embarked on a time-consuming quest.

I have attempted to pay honor to my parents and grandparents by sharing their stories. I would be remiss not to acknowledge the ancestral and historical data provided by my sister Suzanne's husband, Bob Skurda, and the "Dikin Family History" book he and Sue created. It took many hours of research, editing, and printing so we, as a family, could fill in the gaps of our family heritage. Thank you, Bob and Sue.

May this writing fill your heart with understanding and hope.

—James P. Dikin

Introduction

As you peruse down the aisles of the local book store or tinker your fingers searching online for something different to read, you may have come across an obscure book with a catchy title or graphic cover that was pleasing to your senses. You will find that this book is different…to say the least. Some of my friends have asked me "what was my writing style and where would I find the fruits of my labor." That got me to thinking… In what section would a librarian or book seller set me?

I consider this writing a collage of many different types of books and one that probably violates a majority, if not all, of the writing rules that apply to each style of journalism. You see, I am a self-taught writer and have often been told that stories I tell should be put on paper.

I consider myself a man of faith, having been raised by God-fearing parents and in a large family that honored love, unity, community values, and love of our great nation. I dare not hide the fact that God inspires much, if not all, of my words, and if you need His direction, all you need do is follow Him!

This book is not a novel, biography, autobiography, book of poems, songbook, history or educational tool, but then it just might be a collage of all of the above. You also may want to set this book back on the shelf if you have strong discourse with Christian or high family values, humor, and the reality of life itself.

My poems may not follow the rhythm or rhyme of a true poet, and the songs may seem a little dorky, but that's me. My stories are based on my life experiences, and most will bring inspiration and a little humor in a world that is rapidly going down the tubes.

I have grown to accept my literary shortcomings, and I hope that you can too. If you are a journalism purist, this book is not for you, and it may drive you nutz. If punctuation (or lack thereof) drives you to drink, pick up the book again when you get sobered up. I have included the following for purists; !@#$%^&*()_+-={[}]:;"'<,>.?/... put them where you need them!

—Aurel Dikin Sr.
Transcribed and written by my son, Jimmy

PS. The cobbler passed away in 1990, and the love of his life, Dena, followed him three years later. They had been married over sixty-six years and are now together for eternity.

The Cobbler Discovers America

The story begins in the Old World in 1884. My dad was born in Romania and immigrated to a new life in the "Land of Milk and Honey." The promise of a better life is always a strong incentive to make major life changes, and in Pa's case, the desire to be adventurous was in his blood.

Pa, in his day, would be what we'd call a shaker and mover. Pa was going to shake the tree of good fruit until he could catch the sweet plum he longed for. Romania was where he was born, and with few opportunities to offer, he would pursue every one of them with caution while setting deliberate goals.

Pa found that making shoes was an honorable trade and one which could provide an adequate income, while building a product of beauty.

A shoemaker in today's marketplace is usually one who repairs shoes, but back then, the cobbler actually *made* high-quality shoes and boots. They would make a pattern of newspaper from tracing the client's foot or use existing shoes, agree with the purchaser on details of the type and color of finish, and negotiate the cost and date the footwear was needed. They would have the client come in from time to time to assure the fit would be proper (much like women fitting their wedding dresses).

Pa got a lot of training as he embarked on a trade so new to him. He made many mistakes, but they only made him more determined to learn what to do and what not to do on future creations. Pa was young and learned quickly and was well respected for his attention to detail.

With time, an evolution happened in this industry, but that would come many years later. As Pa started out, the tools were simple: a "last" (cast-iron shoe in various sizes to place your upside-down creation on as you near the end of construction); a sharp knife; hammer; a hand-powered leather cutter and skive for tapering the sole leather; an awl, needles; flax; and beeswax. All work was done by hand, making the cobbler's hands and arms very strong from the years of arduous labor.

A treadle-type sewing machine was used for fine seams on thinner leather, but an awl, needle, and thread had to be used on soles. Back then, the strength of the thread for shoemaking could not be bought from the local general store, so the cobbler created his own by spinning flax on his thigh until the needed amount was made for the project.

Back then there were no Velcro fasteners for shoes and boots, but little round buttons with a metal loop for fastening, most commonly used for women's ware.

Trimming the sole leather was done by knife and finished with a piece of broken glass. The edge of raw leather would sport a glazing of hot candle wax being applied. The customer's color choice was then added, and a wax polish was the icing on the leather cake. About color, just like Henry Ford's color choices for his Model-Ts, you could get any color you want, as long its was black.

With the frequent migrating of residents from one European nation to the next, the need for businessmen to become bilingual was a must. Pa had learned several languages and dialects which would be help greatly as he pursued his goal of becoming an American.

Pa was twenty years old when he ventured on his lifelong dream. Coming to America was on the horizon. He traveled to Bremen, Germany, to board the SS *Barbarossa* on March 12, 1904. His twelve-day trip's final destination was Philadelphia, and his port of entry was New York. Pa had saved enough to pay for his own passage, and records indicated he traveled alone and was in good health. Pa worked in the ship's galley and got to know the captain's favorite foods. Records also show that Pa had forty dollars in his wallet when he arrived and, after being processed, was released to his sponsor to continue his journey.

Since Pa was bilingual he assisted many migrants onboard the *Barborossa* with their sometimes-difficult interactions with ship staff. Pa became so respected by the ship's captain that he wanted him to stay onboard as an interpreter to aid future travelers as they ventured their dreams, but he had a goal to pursue.

Pa's plan was to live with his uncle in Philly until he could get oriented and pursue his dream of an independent lifestyle in this large and new country.

Pa's given name was Ioan Jichin, and immigration documents listed him as a single male of Hungarian nationality, and his race as Romanian. It was at the point of entry that Pa had to make the decision. Who he would be in the future? You see, many Old World name formats would not really fit in this new world, so he adopted "John Dikin" as his name. The Dikin name has carried on with respect for five generations.

Pa lived in New York until 1909 and then moved to St. Louis, Missouri. He met a young lady named Irma "Emma" Romonek, and on August 14, 1909, they married. There was a ten-year age difference, but that didn't matter to them; they were determined to embark on a lifelong walk together. At that time, Pa was twenty-four, so that made Ma fourteen… Nowadays, that would not only be frowned upon, but also would be illegal. Some would wonder if such a situation could ever work, but it did. They moved in with relatives in St. Louis, Missouri, and began their new life together.

While in St. Louis, they had four children—Aurel, Julia, Anna, and John Jr.

We lived in St. Louis until I was about fifteen years old, and I worked the night shift with him at the Perfection Biscuit Co. Pa was in the mixing area, and I was baking rolls, bread, and doughnuts. I remember the oven was about a city-block long, and our coffee break was always a time we looked forward to. The guys feeding the line would put a row of empty pans on the conveyor to alert us that the coffee pot was following it. At our end we'd "accidentally" damage a pan or so of bread or rolls and swab them with the butter we used to grease the pans. Oh, it was heaven!

Pa also worked at the Boston Fur and Hide company. Pa was a fur and wool grader and was highly respected for his ability to evaluate, strip, and grade pelts. He could even tell what the animal ate and from what area it came. He did that by simply smelling and feeling the pelt. Some pelts were from hunting or trapping, and some were grown domestically. The condition of the pelt, the preservation, and the expertise the trapper used in skinning it all determined the value.

Pa never did learn how to drive, so at the age of fourteen, I was his chauffer as we traveled state to state. I remember the large sacks used to pack the cotton and wool. They were very big, and we had to jump into the sack to pack down the contents as we loaded them. The downside of having fun were the burrs and ticks that were hiding in the white gold.

From Missouri we moved to Fort Wayne, Indiana.

On September 9, 1944, Pa became a naturalized citizen of the United States of America. Some may ask, "Why did it take so long?" Understanding a country's history and developing the required skills of language and customs ofttimes take years.

The young couple managed to raise a family of eleven children (I was the oldest), forty-one grandchildren, sixty-seven great-grandchildren, and seventy-two great-great-grandchildren. We learned to love, honor, and respect of each other and the community around us.

I was born on Halloween day in 1910. Ma always said I scared the heck out of her, which may be understandable it being the holiday it was and her being a wife and mother as a young midteen. She said her tears of fear changed to tears of joy and happiness as she held me for the first time. I was given the name Aurel (pronounced "O'Dell") and over time took on nicknames, Raleigh or Rollo, which most of my friends called me. I guess Aurel was a type of a weird name, but translations mean many things to those from the Old World. Translation Aurel means "mouth of the lamb." Maybe I didn't cry so much, or maybe it was a word of prophecy that I would be a mouth of the Lamb (Jesus Christ).

This immigrant couple did well, by clinging to their God and to each other through the good times, as well as the bad.

Pa raised us never letting adversity control his destiny. He took on several different vocations, which included fur and wool grading, baking, and in the latter years, shoemaking was his primary way to provide income. In this New World, many of his customers could not afford custom-made shoes, as he had provided in Europe, so Pa specialized in repairing worn-out footwear using his skills as a craftsman, but always using prime and high-quality materials. He believed, "A man is known by the footprint he leaves," which became his advertising motto.

FOREST LAWN Shoe Repair   13046 VAN DYKE

A MAN IS JUDGED BY THE FOOTPRINTS HE LEAVES
J. DIKIN, Proprietor

Pa started the shoemaking business by making custom-made men's slippers in the basement of a house we rented on Montlieu Avenue. He and I also worked at Amby Bakery at Harper and Van Dyke.

Pa's first shoe shop was behind the old Pierson Drugstore on Woodlawn. Later he opened a larger shop on Forestlawn and Van Dyke. I remember Pa would have some of his friends hang out in the back of the shop, and when he was caught up with his work, they would play cards and kibitz as they indulged on  the medicine of choice for the day. One day my younger brother Wally was hanging out at the shop and a young lady came to pick up her repaired shoes and had a toddler in tow. She asked Pa if he had a way to warm up the baby's bottle, and Pa showed her the hot plate, and she was able to soothe the baby with warmed milk. Well, that night when Wally and Pa got home, Wally ran right to Ma and said, "Pa had a pretty girl in the back of the shop." The temperature in the house immediately rose ten degrees and didn't cool down until Pa could explain the situation. Ma was much taller than he and had somewhat the "upper hand" when it came to decision-making. Needless to say, Pa could no longer provide any accommodation if it could be seen inappropriate in any way, shape, or form.

Songs in the Night

The Lord knows the way through the wilderness, and you can change if you want to. You can change; God will help you. You don't have to be the same, you *can change!*

I have seen many changes in my lifetime, but the most memorable is having a father who never complained when things were not going well; he always found a way to provide for the family. I know God was our Provider since, back in those days, there was no such thing as unemployment checks, so with your back against the wall, it was between you and God to fulfill your obligations. Pa would do anything it took to provide for his loving and growing family. Although he couldn't drive, he was quite experienced in changing gears. Years later I was told why he always wanted to have the little kids on his lap. Pa would remove their shoes and feel their feet. You see, along with the eleven of us kids, Pa and Ma also had a son that died of an infection on his heel which would not heal, and finally its seriousness claimed his life. I often wondered what he was thinking while he massaged the little ones' feet.

The Cobbler's Wife

Ma was also an immigrant. Irma (Erma) Romanek was born in Temes Medje, Hungary, and at age thirteen came over with her three brothers on the SS *Laura*, arriving at Ellis Island on May 15, 1908. All four had no money and had to wait until family could vouch and accept them as being their sponsors. Since they were minors, they were held several days until the sponsorship could be arranged and confirmed. The unattended minors had parents already in St. Louis, Missouri, and that was their destination.

Ma met John Dikin while in St. Louis, and within a year, they got married. Back then, weddings were not the grandiose events as they are today, but simple and effective. Families grew, everyone put into the relationship, and the results are evident. When you start out with nothing but love, you have the best start. It was never what you have but what you to contribute to the pot that mattered. Good jobs, money, land, pedigree, and education are all good, but over time, they can all fail. But God never fails. If you love and put God first, everything else will work out.

As I mentioned, Ma was a child-bride, but with so much at stake, and a determination to make a good life for her husband and family, she put all she had into it. The birthing of animals on the farm seemed to be never-ending, as was the growth of our family. Back in those early years, midwives delivered all the babies. It was not uncommon to have two or more taking bottles and needing bathing or changing at one time.

Years later, Ma was able to bring in a woman to help. She was a woman of color, and we learned to respect her, and she learned how to control us kids when Ma or Pa were busy elsewhere. Boy, we tried, but never succeeded in causing her problems. She was always one step ahead, and we would always get caught.

As the family grew, we bonded together to help. There was always so much needing to be done. With each new addition to the family, chores kept increasing in time and effort. Rural life was never easy. Just washing clothes was very hard since the water had to pumped and carried, then be brought to boil on a wood fire; clothes stirred in boiling water, scrubbed on a washboard, drained, twisted, and hung on a line to dry. Also "permanent press" was nonexistent, so if it needed ironing, that was another chore. I, being the oldest, did my fair share of laundry. There was always gardens to till, prep, plant, weed, harvest, and then can, which kept us fed when fresh foods were out of season.

Mom was sweet, but at times, we would test her patience, and that would bring out the Hungarian sternness. Mom never beat us, but when we needed correction, a willow switch was the weapon of choice. I guess the age-old adage "A *switch* in time saves nine" would be a good explanation.

Ma and Pa were Bible-believing folks and taught us to do what is true, honest, loving, compassionate, helpful, and kind.

With a family as big as ours, most of us ended up living in the Metro Detroit Area and for many, many years enjoyed sharing the same church, and our kids found their mates locally, and our family just grew and grew and grew.

Raleigh—the Farmhand

There was a time back in the midtwenties when I had the opportunity to do some honest-to-John farming. You see, being the eldest of twelve kids, it was an easy decision when my parents were asked if I could help a couple living in the country. In this rural area were many family-owned farms, both small and large. My absence from my family would ease the burden somewhat on my parents with one less mouth to feed and less laundry for Ma to do.

I thought it would be a great opportunity to enjoy the fresh country air and experience the freedom and peace of living in a rural community. I didn't have much to pack, so I got my "stuff" together and was picked up by my new employers for a summer of servitude.

The trip seemed to take forever, but back then, the roads were mostly dirt, and the Model-A was doing its best under the circumstances. As we rounded the corner, I saw a somewhat-run-down farmhouse, a barn and a couple of outbuildings, and a large open field being prepared for the season's sugar beet crop. The furrows were not straight, looking much like a bunch of worms lying side by side. The field still had much to plow before the beets could be planted.

As the car stopped and I looked around, I didn't see a tractor, and I soon realized that this couple had a horse-drawn plow, which the old man used to get those squiggly furrows. The horse was an old hag named Bossie that had a sway back, and her general condition was, as they say, "rode hard and put up wet."

I settled in and asked the old man if he had a gun and I'd go out and try to get a rabbit or two for dinner. He handed me a double-barreled, side-by-side shotgun that showed years of use and abuse. The stock looked like it was dropped a lot, and the bluing on the barrels was warn and rusted. I grabbed a handful of shells and headed out to the thicket at the edge of the field. I decided to stand on a stump to get an advantage on the varmints and slipped two shells into the chambers. I snapped the breech closed and awaited my prey. A short time later, Mr. Thumper crossed my path, and I leveled the beast of a gun and pulled the triggers… Yep, I said triggers. The blast of both barrels going off at once was deafening. And if that wasn't enough, my standing on top of a stump was not for long. I landed on my bottom, looking up at the smoke-filled sky and aching all over. My right shoulder hurt because I didn't have the stock butt tight against it, and my butt hurt from landing on another shorter stump that was too close for comfort.

When I got my bearings, I got up and looked around for the hare… It was not there! All I found was a handful of cottontail fur and a mass of unrecognizable meat… That day's hunting was a bust, to say the least, and I was severely reprimanded for wasting shells and not bringing home the bacon.

The next day I helped the old man set up the horse and plow and watched as he began his daily chore of preparing the field. As I watched, I saw that his rows started out quite straight but soon became erratic, and he seemed to frequently cross over the imaginary yellow line. Too soon I was to learn what caused his wavering.

Later that evening, when the sun was about to set, the man's wife was worried because he hadn't returned. She went out to get him for dinner. She came back with just his horse, Bossie, and explained that the old man kept his bottle hidden in a stump at the far end of the field and would visit it each chance he got. That explained the "worm rows," but where was he? She said he was passed out, and she left him there to sleep it off.

I took the harness off the old hag and fed, watered, and brushed her and put her up for the night when I heard yelling and screaming coming from the farmhouse. I ran up from the barn to find the lady badly bruised and crying. The old man wasn't only a drunk, but he was a mean drunk. I wasn't used to this type behavior since my own Pa would have his special libation, but not to the excess, and wasn't mean when he had had a few shots. Pa was a lot smaller than Ma, and I think she would have laid him straight if he got rough with her.

But here, this big, burly man with muscles and rough hands decided to beat his wife senseless for embarrassing him by bringing in Bossie and leaving him out in the field with his bottle. Something inside of me wanted to tear the man from limb to limb, and I minced no kind words with him. I grabbed him by the collar of his shirt and raised my fist and told him, "If you ever hit your wife again, I'll kill you." Anyone that knew me back then knew that a six-foot strapping lad with little on his bones was no match for this Goliath, but even in his drunken stupor, he seemed to understand. During this "intervention," his wife begged me, "Don't hurt him, please don't hurt him, I love him, he'll be okay in the morning."

Well, after that he seemed to better control his attitude, and I'm glad he did. I would have hated to tangle with a man with his strength and size.

The next day was Sunday, and I took Bossie out for a ride. There was no saddle, and Bossie was about fourteen and a half hands high, so I used a stump to get up onto her. It seemed there was always a stump when I needed it—I guess it was a result of the trees being used as fence poles and firewood. Well, my ride took me into a meadow having a blanket of wildflowers. I picked a handful, which I thought might be proper for the occasion, and so I gripped Bossie's mane with my left hand. As I swung over with the flowers in my right hand, it spooked Bossie, and she reared up, throwing me into the abyss, and took off running to the barn. I walked back, put Bossie away, and brought the flowers to the lady of the house.

My summer there was full of hard work, and at harvest-time, I found out what real work was like. Picking sugar beets is backbreaking, and when you lay down at night after a full day of harvesting, the bed felt great, even with the lumpy mattress.

At the end of the season, I got paid. There was a ten-dollar bill and a new suit of clothes. This all happened long before minimum wage, child labor laws, and other current considerations for youthful labor. I returned home to the noise, confusion, and love that I missed during the summer as a farmhand.

Are You There?

One day I was in deep thought and found myself looking back to what happened in my life. Years have come and gone, so many—and so fast. I asked myself, "What have I accomplished since 1924, when I was fourteen years old and in the eighth grade?"

As the eldest of eleven children, I had no idea what the future had in store for me. I was just entering my teen years and found it my responsibility to help my dad. There was so much that had to be done, and like him, I shouldered chores to keep up with the needs of a growing family.

The school bus picked us up for the long drive to school, and when we were ready to go home, it was another long trip. Many chores had to be done before supper, so homework had to be done later, leaving little time to play during the week. Our weekends allowed some time to have fun, but there were always chores to do even then.

At that time, graduation from the eighth grade was a benchmark in life, but I had fallen behind in my grades. I didn't want to be a disappointment to my parents, although I felt that I did as good as I could in studying and doing homework.

My younger sister Julia was a year younger than me, and I was in the same grade as her.

One night about midnight, it seemed I was drawn outside to the middle of the barnyard. I looked upward, and the sky was clear, and the stars looked like diamonds on a black tablecloth. I gazed into the heavens in awe. It was late October, and the harvest moon was shining to its fullest.

Somehow, I felt I needed to say something, and looking up, I said, "God, they say that you are up there, but I have never spoken to You before. I believe You have control over the sun, moon, and stars. I need to know if You are there, and if You are Who they say You are, You will hear me. I need to graduate, and if You let me do so, I want not to have grades less than my younger sister. If this happens, I will know You have heard me, and I will never smoke a cigarette." You may think this is no big thing, but for years, I saw my father struggle with smoking which, later in life, caused his death by lung cancer. Many of dad's friends smoked, and I was tempted to follow my father's actions.

Graduation time has come, and now for the test. The questions were hard, and I did my best, with hope and anticipation. Maybe there was a little doubt, but then this was something new for me.

After the final exam, we had to wait two weeks for the results to be mailed to our parents. I guess they didn't trust us kids to carry home a letter that might not get to your mom and dad.

One day the envelopes came to the mailbox.

Julia said, "I have my report card."

I asked her, "What did you get?"

She said, "91.9, what did you get?"

I opened my envelope, and mine was "91.9."

It was the same exact score as she had, not even one-tenth percent lower or higher. You see, I asked not to be below her; I didn't say equal or above her. God gave me exactly what I petitioned Him for.

At that exact moment, I realized without a doubt that there is a God, and He does answer prayers.

Years later I had an occasion to be tested. Pa had left his cigarettes and matches on the dresser, and as I walked passed, I grabbed them and headed to the seclusion of the attic. I removed one out of the pack, and holding it in one hand, I lit a match with the other and was about to light the cigarette. Standing there, I heard an audible voice saying, "I kept my promise. Will you keep yours?"

I snuffed the smoldering temptation and knew with certainty that God is, indeed, a God that I could depend on. He is watching over me, and He is the strength I need and expects us to always keep our commitments to Him.

That all happened a few years back, when I was a teenager, and now I am eighty-six years old. I never smoked, and I believe my obedience and commitment have rewarded me many times over with good health and prosperity.

God is good, and his mercy endureth forever!

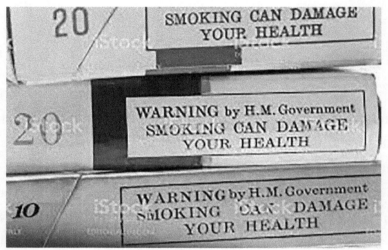

(Getty Images)

My Rum-Running Friend

I would like you to meet a friend of mine. You see, Johnny Z. and I kind of grew up together, and we had a lot in common. We both came from large families, and we were both thin and tall and had a little bit of the wild side that would spring up every now and then. One major difference was that I had a meeting with my Maker and Johnny did not. I wanted him to know the Lord as I was learning to know Him. Johnny told me, "Money is my God." This really hurt, and I told him, "Johnny, someday my God is going to take your god away from you." Little did I know, those words would become words of prophecy from a young man as I began my long walk with God.

We would go places together and pal around. Johnny had a beautiful new car that was jet-black. It was always shined up, and riding around with him boosted my humble stature. Everyone knows, flashy dressing and sporting a fancy car is a magnet to attract girls. Johnny would stop in at Pa's shoe shop to pick up a large tin of shoe polish. "Griffin" kept his shoes polished and also doubled as car wax. Boy, that car shined like no other!

One day I found out how Johnny could afford his black beauty. He was never the type guy to follow the law, and his steps always took him at least one foot over the line. He made friends with the underworld, and as prohibition was in full swing, he found running rum from Port Huron to Detroit was a great way to make his car payments. Johnny would haul cabbage in burlap sacks from the farms near the Saint Clair River where the illegal booze came across from Canada. He found he could smuggle the bottles hidden in the sacks of cabbage, and that way people needing vegetables and a bit of the medicinal tonic were very happy.

One day at his house, when no one was home, he asked me to visit his basement to see his gun collection. He had a footlocker filled with handguns and ammunition. As I looked at the stash, my eyes widened. There were so many guns. Some were pearl-handled revolvers, some had wooden grips, and he even had a couple of German Luger automatics. He said, "Hey, Raleigh, let's have a little fun." With that he stood up an old mattress against the basement wall, and we attached some targets. We popped rounds for about an hour until we realized the vast amount of smoke we were creating. So we opened the windows, straightened up, and found that a mattress does not stop a bullet.

The holes in the wall would be hard for Johnny to explain to his parents. Before I left, Johnny told me to take any gun I wanted. A pearl-handled .38 caught my eye, and as I inspected it, I noticed that the serial number had been filed off. What I did see was, "Detroit Police Department" was stamped on its barrel, and I asked Johnny how he got them. He said that the guy he worked for would give him a new gun for each run to the boarder so if he had a problem, the cops could not tie him to other smuggling cases.

I took my prize home to the farm and would target practice with my new toy. It was so cool. Then one day I was in the kitchen and I was cleaning my gun of all residue from breaking bottles. I wasn't schooled in gun safety, and as I haphazardly started cleaning it, my gem went off in my hands. My younger sister Julia was standing just a few feet from me, and the bullet missed her by inches. Thinking back, I know God had protected my little sister and was showing me that the gun wasn't worth the danger that I brought to family. I immediately took it outside and grabbed the axe and smashed it on the well head. Then I buried it.

Someday a teenager with metal detector, looking for treasures on that old farm, will come across a rusted, smashed, pearl-handled .38 with "Detroit Police Department" on its barrel and no serial number. He will post it on e-Bay as an oddity, and it will probably bring a good bid.

Well, one day Johnny came over with his "black beauty," but it looked different. It wasn't shiny anymore. The wheel rims had been repainted, and there were bullet holes just behind the driver's seat. It seemed that Johnny's last trip got him too close to the law. They were hot on his trail, and when bullets started flying, Johnny decided he'd better change his vocation. This was the start of Johnny's decline, which never seemed to stop.

Johnny became an excellent welder, but one day a spark put out his right eye. With only one good eye, he had a hard time getting, or keeping, a job. With a wife and kids to support, Johnny would do just about any kind of job, just for food. The trials in his life led him into alcoholism, and he smoked heavily. In his final years, Johnny Z. drove an old, beat-up four-door sedan with full-size acetylene and oxygen tanks lying across the back seat with hoses and torches jammed on the floorboard. With a trunk full of wire coat hangers, he would search for work, to no avail. You see, although he was an excellent welder, he could not afford the tools of the trade. Proper welding rods cost money, so he used coat hangers. Johnny would work for beer and smokes, and his family suffered a life of poverty.

God has blessed me and my family beyond all what could be imagined and provided many opportunities for me to help Johnny and his family in times of need.

Johnny's black beauty took him down a road that led him to a prison of pain and suffering.

My God will have no other god before Him…ever!

> Thou shalt have no other gods before me. (Exodus 20:3, KJV)

A Fair to Remember

"What do you want to do this summer?" my Uncle Frank asked. I knew what I wanted, and that was to have an adventure, but my mind drifted back to some of the "adventures" I had over the years with Frank.

Frank was a daredevil. He kept drawing me into some of his shenanigans, which would often result in someone getting hurt, but would provide fodder for gut-wrenching laughter. I remembered the time he dared me to jump from one roof level of a shed to the lean-to below. I challenged him to go first. Well, the roof of the lean-to wasn't as strong as he thought, and he ended up caught around his waist with sharp-edged slivers injected in his peri-abdomen.

Then there was the time we were at the rail yard just doing what we do…and he got on top of another shed and decided to jump unto a pile of black sand. Well, it wasn't sand but a pile of cooling ash from a steam engine which had dumped its load hours before. The gut-wrenching scream was probably heard in the next county. He was treated with lard and butter to try to ease the burn, but I think that cured him from shed-jumping.

These memories of fun days with Frank were interrupted by him again asking, "What we were going to do this summer." I said, "Well, the World's Fair is on in Chicago, why don't we go and see what it's all about."

The 1933 World's Fair was being advertised as "A Century of Progress." We busied ourselves getting all the information possible to make this "once in a lifetime" road trip. Uncle Frank was about the same age as me, so we would spend free time together. We had no problem assembling clothes; we didn't have many to select from, so the choices were "fairly" easy. We pooled our funds, but that wasn't hard either…neither of had much to throw into the pot. We couldn't afford to drive, not having a reliable car or funds for gas and maintenance, so we decided to hitchhike. Boy, were we going to have fun. The money we were going to save on transportation we could spend at the fair. We didn't even think about where we would stay but thought we'd cross that bridge when we came to it. The day of departure came, and we said our goodbyes to family and started our cross-country adventure.

We hooked rides with some helpful motorists, who all seemed intrigued in our "adventure in progress." They were all envious and wished they could tag along. As the miles passed and the helpful chauffeurs had to make turns from our designated route, we finally got a ride from a chicken farmer hauling his flock to market.

The old man in his bib overalls and straw hat seemed friendly enough, but we soon found out why. He kept drinking from his open bottle of whiskey, and his cigars started making us oozy. It was when he kept swerving all over the Westbound lane on a two-lane highway that we asked him to stop, and we politely relocated to the rear of the truck. You need to close your eyes and envision two semi-well-dressed and fairly good-looking young men sitting on the rear of a chicken truck. Then the fun started. We didn't realize that the aerodynamics of the situation would provide a continual shower of "foul" feathers and foul weather from their drippings. Well, that was the final straw! In tandem we jumped off the next time he slowed down a little.

We again sought the help of passing cars. The drivers were friendly enough, but often commented on our choice of colognes. Finally, we wheeled into Chicago. The town is bustling. Frank and I tidied up in the restroom of a gas station. Some of the feathers were missed, and as we did our picking from each other and looked at the mirror on the wall of this dilapidated restroom, we got a view of a couple of guys down on their luck. We did our best, and after washing the chicken goop from our hair, we dried up to meet the world as reformed hobos.

We headed to the fair, and our eyes widened at the sight. It was sooooo big. As we went from display to display, seeing things we had only dreamed of, there were cars of all makes and models. Not only those made in our Motor City but those from around the world. Then there were industrial displays and household appliances of every type, make, and model. There were street vendors hacking their wares and food to satisfy any pallet. We selected the cheapest to calm the gurgling in our stomachs and then moved on to the entertainment area. The rides were awesome. Back in Detroit, we only saw rides like these in the magazines, but here we were walking among them. We rode a couple just to lay credence to our trip. The rides drew us closer to some of the beauties, but that closeness was not always appreciated by them. We must have smelled like chicken farmers, so we decided that viewing the beauty from afar would be wise. I had to keep Frank in line so he wouldn't make a fool of himself. He was good at that.

As night fell and the day's adventure came to a close, we chose a couple of park benches to rest our weary bodies. It was a long and stressful trip, and the fair had drained every ounce of energy out of us, but the restful night was not to be. About 2:00 a.m., a beat cop—who stood over six feet with shoulders as wide as a broomstick—was touring the park and sadistically whacking the soles of unsuspecting park occupants with his billy club. We heard the screams of those down the path and quickly gathered our senses and belongings and headed for the woods. We found trees to sit against to complete our disrupted sleep and in the morning decided to start heading back to our homes.

We again got a few short-distance rides in passenger vehicles but soon ended on foot. Our shoes were doing okay—I guess it was the attention I gave them before we left. Having a shoemaker as your father, and with my own personal shoemaking abilities, our walking was endurable. I'm sure those others at the park, who were rapped by King Kong, weren't walking quite as well this morning.

About halfway home, and between rides, we came along a farm that was growing watermelons. With stomachs gurgling again, we decided to pick one to calm the pain. Frank and I broke it and, after eating most of it, used the rest to wash our hands. We didn't have dry-wipes or water available, so wouldn't the watermelon juice suffice? Bad decision. The stickiness and sugar drew all the flies and bees to share our ill-found treasure. It was probably God's reminder of the law (not of supply and demand), "Thou shall not steal."

Soon, in the distance, we heard a truck coming. It was a noisy truck. It was a car hauler deadheading back to the Motor City. *Deadheading* means "riding empty." Just think about it. That truck had probably carried some of those Motor City gems to the fair, and Frank and I would be honored to ride in this truck. The driver offered to give us a ride, but we would have to ride in the trailer since his company had rules about not allowing passengers. That was okay with us... Just get us home! That watermelon wasn't sticking to our ribs, and we were longing for some of Ma's cooking. That had to be a ride that put our chicken ride to shame. An empty trailer, with bad shocks and loose chains bouncing all over, shook us to no end, and the noise was almost unbearable. Hours later we saw our beloved "You are Entering the City of Detroit" sign. We took a few short, free rides and finally got home. For years we reminisced of our Chicago trip and were so blessed when the state fair was set up in Ferndale and our road trips were less eventful.

A Walk in the Garden
(We Are the Salt of the Earth)

As I look back on the decades of my life that God has given me, I remember the countless hours I had spent in my gardens. I loved my roses and loved bringing the aroma into my love when the blooms were ready. Dena also loved plants and always had all types of greenery throughout the house.

I would plant, cultivate, and fertilize the roses, and God provided the increase. The Jackson and Perkins Hawaiian rose was one of my favorites. The coloration and the sweet berry aroma was pleasant to the eyes and nose. The stems were long and straight. I guess because they were called Hawaiian, I was drawn to that line, but all in all, they were awesome roses.

It seems like, as busy as I always was, I still had plenty of time to tend my gardens. I had vegetables and a few fruit trees. I preferred natural fertilizer and remember the time I had a load of fresh cow doodle delivered. I used what I needed for the garden and had the boys spread the rest on the grass. That weekend we had a very heavy rain and the lawn was very slippery. The irregular distribution of the manure left patches of beautiful green turf, surrounded by not-so-pretty brown spots. I also learned early on that horse manure is not too good for a garden. Their digestive system lets many grains pass through, and you are blessed with a bumper-crop of rye, oats, and other "weeds" between your veggies.

I had many different gardens, and I even made a tiered rock garden in front of my shoe shop. It helped me save space but also made it easier to maintain having some higher than ground level.

I also realized that someone with a green thumb does not get it because he knows what to plant, how to plant it, or how to take care of it, but rather he gets his green thumb from weeding his garden.

The solace I got from gardening was muchly because of my quiet time with my Creator. He and I talk a lot, and I had found that early in the morning, before most of the world awakes from their slumber, was an ideal time with Him as I cultivated or weeded my prided veggies.

I remember a song I would sing to Him. It was sung by Jim Reeves, and others, and is called "I Come to the Garden Alone."

> I come to the garden alone
> While the dew is still on the roses
> And the voice I hear falling on my ear
> The Son of God discloses.
> Refrain:
> And He walks with me, and He talks with me,
> And He tells me I am His own;
> And the joy we share as we tarry there,
> None other has ever known.

He speaks, and the sound of His voice,
Is so sweet the birds hush their singing,
And the melody that He gave to me
Within my heart is ringing.
Refrain:
And He walks with me, and He talks with me,
And He tells me I am His own;
And the joy we share as we tarry there,
None other has ever known.
I'd stay in the garden with Him
Though the night around me be falling,
But He bids me go; through the voice of woe
His voice to me is calling.
Refrain:
And He walks with me, and He talks with me,
And He tells me I am His own;
And the joy we share as we tarry there,
None other has ever known.

Many times, I found solutions to my daily problems whether they be family, job, finances, or whatever by spending time on my knees, pulling weeds, and talking to my "Best Friend." We are the salt of the earth; therefore, whatever we make from the fruits of our harvests need not be salted...

Lord of Life, I Pray You

Enlighten my mind to know the remedies
For my patient's ills and touch my heart
To feel compassion for their suffering
Let me heal them with a portion of *Your*
wisdom
And power, and when I cannot heal them
Let me help them on at least to a deeper faith
And resignation in Your love
Amen

When visiting a new doctor for the first time, I said, "Sir, I believe in prayer. I will be praying for you, that you will have wisdom and compassion in helping me with my problem."

He said for me to follow him. We went into the hall where he showed me a large picture with the above words on it. I found that the doctor knew exactly what I was talking about, and he would be guided by the hand of God.

My Prayer
(Inspired by God…written by His child)

I did not ask for fame or glory
I did not ask for houses or land
I only asked for Your true mercy
And to be led by Your dear hand.
When I approached Your throne of mercy
With humble heart I came
Asking to know Your will, dear Lord
To be a servant known by Thy name
Gold and silver, I need not, Lord
Wealth and fame are not for me
Just let me place my hand in Thine
That I may know that I am pleasing Thee
When you pray, be very careful
You do not pray amiss
Self must bow to His will
The Lord is pleased in this
(Aurel Dikin Sr.)

The Potter and the Clay

On Sunday morning, as I was returning home after opening the church for the day's services, I happened to turn on the car's radio, and a minister was talking about "the potter and the clay." I turned off the radio. I said, "Lord, I'm going to turn off this radio, I have heard enough from man about this subject, now I want to hear what You have to say." While driving, I turned the radio off and meditated on the Lord to try to fully understand the true meaning of the potter and the clay. The Lord enlightened my soul with the following:

First, the potter must take the clay out of the earth, as clay and sand do not mix. Both clay and sand have their own specific properties and on their own have their own specific use but, mixed together, do not bond together well. The same parallel is applied when the Lord saves us and takes us out of the earth for Himself. We are still in the world but are not part of the world.

The second step is when the potter selects the clay and starts to make a mold for himself. He works and works on the clay to make it pliable for the image he wants to create. The Lord works and works on us to perfect us into His image, for we are His workmanship, created in Christ Jesus. At first the clay is hard and does not respond well to the potter's hands, but after much work and patience, the clay starts to take shape.

The third step is the most difficult one for the potter. The vessel is formed from the inside out, then a top is made.

Ofttimes the forming is done during a spinning process. Have you ever thought you were going around in circles? When the vessel is properly formed, the potter carefully places it into the fiery furnace to harden it to prepare it for use and stand the test of all his hard work. After the Lord saves us, He puts us into the fiery furnace of life to see if we, too, will stand the test of life. First Peter 1:7 tells us that the trial of our faith is more precious than gold that perishes, though it be tried with fire. It is to say that Christians cannot stand this first test and become broken vessels, unfit for the Master's use.

It is interesting to note that when the clay is ready, a mold is made. The potter then works on the image from the inside out. In the same manner, the Lord works on us from the inside out, removing the impurities that exist in us and forms us to for the specific use He has for us. This is a very careful process because the potter knows that once the mold is made and a top placed on it, the vessel can no longer be reformed unless he breaks the vessel.

After the fiery furnace, the vessel is removed carefully and examined for any cracks. These cracks, whether large or small, will weaken the vessel and cause it to fail, even under normal use. When he is assured that no cracks exist, he is now ready to adorn the outside with his beautiful image and place his name on the bottom. You see, He wants others to see His image and be drawn to Him by seeing that image in your life. When others see the beauty of your life, they will then search for the name of the Potter Who created you into who you have become. The

Potter then places you back into the furnace to seal His image and His stamp of approval, preparing you through more trials and tests so you will be "meet for the Master's use."

A beautiful vessel properly formed and without imperfections is useless until something is put into it. At this point, a Christian is useless until he receives the precious Holy Spirit. But just receiving it is not enough…he must be willing to let the Master fill him to overflowing and let Him pour of this precious gift to others seeking a drink from the river of life.

In the process of pouring, the vessel may become old, worn, bruised, and nicked, but since it was created by the Great Potter, it will still be valuable for His use. Old vessels in this day and age are valuable and very precious.

Isn't it wonderful how we, too, can be poured out vessels as for the Lord, fit for the Master's use? We, too, will have nicks and bruises as we become poured out for our Lord and Savior as we become fruitful in the kingdom of God.

An Open Book

I always desired that my life would be like an open, well-written book so that as those around me would take me off the shelf and open me up, they could read how my God has moved in and through me. My hope has been that my life's book not be science fiction or a romance novel, but rather one of a more educational and spiritual writing.

As I peruse my book in my mind, I see many chapters and so many words. I never did keep a journal, but God has gifted me with a memory of the many challenges, tests of faith and blessings which He bestowed on me and my family.

The book is unique. It is packed with page after page, all having footnotes for scriptural references which He brought to my remembrance for each and every entry. The historical documentary would help my parents understand why I was the type of kid I was and later in life help my wife and kids know the reason for my existence. As you get three-quarters of the way through it, you'll find that the rest of the book is just blank pages, which will also be written as life goes on.

I always guarded my heart, knowing the Heavenly Father was watching, and it was my desire to please Him, knowing that a "testimony" can only exist if there is a "test" and many times "money" may be involved…therefore being a testimony.

God has kept each and every promise in my life. There was a time when the presbytery of our church prophesied over me, and as I read it decades later, found during a simple spirit-filled service, a plan was formed for my life by my Heavenly Father and was happening without me knowing. The Word says,

> Eye has not seen, nor ear heard, Nor have entered into the heart of man The things which God has prepared for those who love Him. (1 Corinthians 2:9)

What's in a Name?

Aurel
Root—Aurelin, "voice of the lamb"
French/Latin—gold
Expression—flirting comes naturally to him
Personality—someone who is socially inclined
Natural—artistic and intellectual
Emotional—when he is in nature, he is completely happy
Character—versatile, dual-natured, and likes change
Physical—a brave man
Mental—a good education is important to him
Motivation—self-reliance in himself is not lacked
Born—October 31, 1910

Dena
Root: Adena
Hebrew—sensuous, voluptuous
Personality—she has a sweet disposition
Natural—very genteel and kind to others
Emotional—many tears she has smiled away

Physical—her eyes change with her moods

Mental—a bold and wise counselor

Motivation—she tries to always do her best

Lives by—Proverbs 22:6

Born—March 6, 1914

Faith and Myrtle

Faith was the oldest. As I mentioned, we lost our baby Dena Mae at eighteen months, and with faith in God our Father, we decided to have another child. The name Faith is a strong name and signifies anticipation of things to come.

Faithy was Dena's right hand as our family grew and grew. Maintaining a household that produced additions about every two years was a handful.

Music was always a family tradition, and with Faith, it was cello and French horn. Her musical abilities included the concert band and the marching band. After graduation she was in the church choir for many years. In high school Faithy learned how to write shorthand, which helped her land a job with Chrysler Corp. as a secretary.

I remember our times around our very large kitchen table. The seating arrangements were simple—Dena to my left, then Richard, then Myrtle, at the end opposite me was Faith, then Suzie, then Junior, then Jimmy (at my right hand and under the wall-mounted telephone).

Our evening dinners were always a time of good food, a rehash of the interesting daily happenings, and a joke or two. Like I said, I am usually a no-mess type of man, and I could always control the situation at hand just by clearing my throat.

This one night it was getting quite rambunctious, and I cleared my throat to restore order… It didn't come. Faithy kept things going, so I again did my "throat call to order," still no improvement. I then took a forkful of mashed potatoes and flipped them to the opposite end of a six-foot table, and they landed squarely on Faith's glasses. Everyone roared as the white mushy mess dripped down her face. I think we were still laughing at bedtime.

Faith lived home with us until 1969 and helped by contributing to the household finances. She married Garry Cooper that year, and they later adopted a baby boy.

Myrtle was one year younger than Faith. Born in 1937, she, too, followed her older sister's path of education by also learning how to write shorthand. Both Faith and Myrtle had help with their homework in that regard since Dena knew this unique and now-somewhat-obscure type of speed-writing. In the music area, Myrtle played violin and flute and was also in the concert and marching bands. Myrtle joined her sister and spent many years in the church choir.

Myrtle also lived at home while working at the Dodge Truck Plant as a secretary in the purchasing department.

Beyond her extended financial contributions to the household budget, Mert was our family chauffer. Faith didn't drive till many years later, so anyone going anywhere knew who could do it.

I remember the black 1949 Plymouth Sedan she had. What a bucket of bolts, but it ran. Boy, did it run!

One day Mert and Faith were tooling around, and she had to make a quick stop. Till this day, I still don't know what the distraction was, but her sudden stop threw Faith forward, then forcefully backward, and broke the seat back on the passenger side. Picture this—Faith riding lying down as they drove into the drive. This was the evening's funny happening for the day… No mashed potatoes tonight.

Then there was the vacation we took to a friend of mine's cabin in Baraga (in the Upper Peninsula). Chuck said we could use his cabin for free if we would do him a favor. He needed a well pit dug so he could build a small block room for his well pump.

It seemed like a doable project, so we packed up the brood and headed north. Without the current interstates, or higher speed limits, the trip seemed to take forever. If that wasn't enough, since the Big Mac Bridge was just a dream at that time, you had to take a ferry across the Straits of Mackinaw.

Would you believe it, the ferries were on strike, and we had to spend hours parked in the holding lot until the boats started running again.

We took two cars since Mert and Faith also brought along a couple of their girlfriends. The one car was a borrowed Woody station wagon and there was our not-so-trusty family car. Under the best conditions it still would have been a difficult trek, but conditions change…sometimes they just keep getting worse.

Under the extreme load our car was carrying, old Betsy decided to blow her clutch while going up a steep hill. We happened to find a local mechanic, but he was crippled, so I had to do all the work with his coaching.

Then it was time to dig the infamous well pit. Such an easy task should have only taken an hour or two. Not so! The ground was gray clay, and you had to use a second shovel to scoop off the clay from the first. Then it rained…and rained… and rained. The half-dug pit became a swimming hole, and every shovel of mud was a slimy mess.

All was not gloom and doom. We did find the fishing hole and brought home the bacon.

Myrtle married Dennis Gentry in 1971 and in later years also adopted, but theirs being a baby girl.

Richard, My Oldest Son

As often happens when two people love each other, and both coming from large families, after the loss of Dena Mae, and the births of Faith and Myrtle, Dena and I decided to again add to the Dikin clan. Richard was born in March of 1942.

Dick was our first of three sons, and as such there was somewhat of a learning process raising a boy. The girls were all sweet and mellow; then here comes a little fireball with so much energy and being so different from his sisters.

I remember there was a time I was dead against firearms in the house. I guess it was from the accidental discharge of a revolver that almost hit my sister Julia, or maybe it was the serious rear-end collision which killed my hunting dogs when I was going out for birds one day with a friend. In any case, I had my rules.

In the early family days there was no TV, only a radio, which provided hours of audio stories with a full background of special effects to set your imagination in high gear. Again, I had my rules. I told the kids, "You can listen to anything on the radio, but if shooting starts…turn it off."

One day Richard turned on the old tube-type radio with the intention of hearing a good story. The music began and played the *William Tell Overture*. It was the introduction to *The Lone Ranger* series. Then we heard, "Hi-Ho Silver, Away," followed by a horse whinnying and then four distinct gunshots.

Many of you remember the TV series with the Lone Ranger and Tonto. They were good guys, right? Well, I guess I was the bad guy because I heard the radio click off and Dick mumble, "It's just not fair, the program didn't even start yet."

Then on his fifth birthday, Dena had a little party for him, allowing him to invite some of his friends. When he unwrapped the gift from one of his buddies, there it was…a belt with two holsters which had two pearl-handled revolver cap guns. Dick was happy to see them, but knew how I would feel about them.

After all the boys left, I took Dick aside to have a talk about the gift and why I had such strong feelings about guns. I believe the Lord gave me the words to say, but I told him, "If you will put these guns in the trash bag, I will go out and buy you something much nicer. He was reluctant at first, but I think he knew that I was a dad that could be trusted. The next day I went out and bought him a real nice jig saw (nowadays they call them scroll saws). I showed him how to take pages out of magazines, glue them to a piece of Masonite, and cut them into jigsaw puzzles. His buddies thought it was the cat's meow. After that, he and his friends spent much of their spare time making puzzles and other projects.

As Richard got older, he had the hankering to take girls out. We had to test the waters—and had to add cold water (and even ice cubes) when the water got too hot.

Dick was quite energetic when it came time to start driving. He would do most anything just to get the keys to the family car every now and then. One time I remember how he changed the oil, and it wasn't until later, when I went to the store, I saw the idiot light tell me the filter wasn't tightened and all my new oil was in my rearview mirror. Then the time Dick tuned up the station wagon—he yanked all the plug wires without labeling them as to where they went…had to call my mechanic Chuck for rewiring advice.

One day Dick decided to detail the bucket of bolts by washing and waxing the exterior. Before I knew it, he had pulled all the trim so he could do a super job, but halfway through it he forgot he had a date planned. For a couple of days, I had a weird-looking set of wheels. It was almost like a girl putting on only half her makeup.

Dick joined up with the City of Warren Police band. He had been playing the slush-pump (trombone) throughout junior high and high school, and he enjoyed wearing a police band uniform and playing in parades and such.

Richard joined the Air Force Reserves and served his committed time. He met the love of his life, Janice, married, and they had four kids. Janice was from Kentucky, and their family trips to the South were very appealing to him, plus he wanted to fulfill dreams of country living.

Dick was a hard worker (hmm, don't know where he got that from), so they moved South to the Symsonia area. Later they took on the dream of making a former barn into their "dream house."

In May of 1977, Richard called and shared how the barn repurposing was coming and invited Dena and me down for a little "vacation." I offered to bring a trailer load of power tools, thinking that a little extra muscle and the right tools might move his project to completion.

We took the long trip in a foreign land, and as we rolled up to their barn house, Dick met us at the car.

He said, "Dad, I called, and you and Mom had already left, and I couldn't reach you. I have been feeling very sick, and I thought you may have wanted to stay home."

Well, Richard's illness seemed to get worse and worse by the day. The symptoms where much like the flu, but within a week, he was hospitalized and soon passed away. The disease was such that one by one his organs were shutting down, and this small country town's medical team had never seen this type of rapid downturn. The actual cause of the illness was only identified weeks after his funeral by blood samples being sent and tested in Okinawa, where the CDC had specialized labs for identifying unique diseases. They said it was "Rocky Mountain tick fever."

Here Dena and I were, hundreds of miles from the rest of our family and friends, and it was also to be a special time for Dena and Janice with the upcoming Mother's Day on the horizon. Mother's Day…

I called Brother James Beall back home, and my broken heart was hardly allowing the words to come out. Brother Jim knew Dick from the day he was born. He dedicated him as a baby, watched him grow, confirmed him at age eleven, married him and Janice, and dedicated all four of their kids.

When we finished praying and absorbing his words of comfort, he asked, "Rollo, do you want me to come down?" I said, "No, it's way too far." I guess there must have been a nudge from God because he said, "I'll be right there." Brother Jim came down with his sister Pat and her husband, Pete.

The little country funeral home was packed with family and friends. I never saw a beard as the one Dick had grown; it was pitch-black and down to his chest. His curly hair was a Dikin trademark and matched his beard.

As Brother Jim officiated, he reminisced the growing years of my eldest son and the twinkle he always had in his eyes. It was that sense of adventure that brought him South and opened doors of opportunity and desire to create a unique home for his family.

My kids all came down for the funeral, and the common bond of love and comfort we all shared gave meaning to "the ties that bind."

Jimmy went to the local barber, and she almost lost it. You see, for many years, Dick and Jim looked like twins and were frequently called by each other's name. But here was someone who knew Dick passed away, then saw almost an exact duplicate, only without a beard.

After the funeral I took Dena to Hawaii for a time of regrouping our feelings and remembering our son in private. When we came back, the hurt seemed to return when we walked in to find that Jimmy was starting to grow a beard too. He looked so much like Dick, and I know I wasn't easy on him about it. Jim stood his ground, saying he liked the look, so in time we got used to it. Cookie dusters and chest bibs are personal and, if maintained, properly add character to someone's character.

Jimmy, Aurel Jr., and Suzanne

Jimmy is our second-oldest son and, like all three sons, had spent a lot of time with me working, fishing, and doing "what we do." The boys would go with a wagon throughout the neighborhood picking up old newspapers from our neighbors and bringing them to my shoe shop where I had a corner set up for them. I had a friend from church which had a steel-and-chrome polishing business. He needed newspapers to be fully opened, shiny paper and flyers removed, then rolled in stacks about two-inch high and tied with twine. Pop Baer used the paper to wrap his finished product and paid about twenty dollars per ton to whoever would produce it.

This was quite a chore, but the boys got a little cash out of each delivery.

Jimmy, like all the others, played instruments also. He played trumpet, baritone, and French horn. And when I wasn't looking, he played hooky… Just kidding! Jim started playing trumpet when he was in the fifth grade and was in concert bands, the dance band, and the marching band. He also was in the church choir for over eleven years.

Jimmy seemed to be a real go-getter, never letting anything stand in his way as he met the business world head-on.

It seems his abilities abounded in the computer industry with being able to operate and manage equipment and people from first-generation systems to those of the state-of-the-art type at the time he retired from Burroughs. He worked in banking, construction, for an engineering firm, was a city manager in Georgia, and a resident manager for a senior high-rise.

Jimmy met, and later married, Jeanie, and they have three kids.

Aurel Raieigh Dikin Jr. was born in 1948. Named after me, Junior also spent much time by my side helping and learning.

I remember a go-cart he made. Oh, it had all the bells and whistles on it. It had a surrey top, clay plant pots on the front as headlamps, and even a discarded telephone and cord—I guess AT&T got their wireless ideas from him.

Junior and I didn't always see things the same way, and in his teen years, we both had a lot of growing up to do. I remember one time he had left home to live with a buddy. One day he came home with orange hair—I guess it might have been a dyeing gone wrong, or maybe it was just in style.

Junior's musical skills were in the use of an accordion. He plays accordion and piano, and when I got an organ for the family, he would sit down and tickle the ivories.

Junior's business skills are mainly in wheeling and dealing. He has been known to horse-trade, buy short and sell long, and be able to barter for the most obscure item, just to sell it the next day.

Raleigh's expertise is in real estate, and he has also taught higher education classes for new and recertifying real-estate agents.

Junior was married twice. Mary Jane and Ellen each have one girl.

Suzanne Marie was born in 1949. Suzie is the baby of the clan and so different from the rest of us. We all have brown hair and brown eyes; she is a blue-eyed blond-haired girl. She didn't take much to music (except being in the church choir), but she had other abilities.

At a young age, Suzie learned how to twirl a baton… So she did! Every marching band had one, and we had ours.

Sue married Bob Skurda in 1976, and they have two children.

Sue and Bob were heavily involved in the children's ministry for many years at our church. In the areas of organization, preparation for events, making stage backdrops and teaching God's Word, they proved their love and commitment to the kids, the church, and their Heavenly Father. Their involvement grew in many other aspects of ministry within the fellowship.

Also, Suzanne and Bob are the Dikin family historians and have researched and published the Dikin legacy of family and life events.

Our Up North Cottage
A Quiet Place in the Woods

Our cottage had its beginning, quite by accident, in 1959. For years we were guests of relatives who were building a cottage in the Roscommon, Michigan area. Back in those days, everyone seemed to want to help others as they put their muscle and meager funds into play. Family bonds were strengthened as trees came down, firewood split, foundations poured, and walls built. Before you knew it, a roughed-in structure became a work in progress, and an acceptable shelter until the next step of the project.

In July of '59, Dena and I wanted to take the younger kids up North, but we knew that Pat and Pete had Pastor Beall up there on vacation, and we were very determined *not* to disrupt her solitude. This was not in the liking of the kids. We had a favorite swimming beach on Higgins Lake at Gerrish Township Park, Higgins was such a peaceful lake back then. This was the time before high-speed powerboats, pontoons as big as the *Queen Elizabeth*, and personal watercraft that sprout rooster tails forty feet in the air.

Although our kids were well-seasoned campers, having experienced Boy and Girl Scout outings, Dena and I always enjoyed the softness of a bed off the ground. We decided to camp at the Sportsman's Camp in Mio, far enough away from the tempting swimming hole. I had a Plymouth station wagon, which I fitted with bedding in the rear for mom and me. Suzie slept across the front seat, and Jimmy and Junior in a small pup tent. It was a typical summer in Northern Michigan…*not!*

The daytime temperature was eighty-four degrees, and at night it was forty-eight degrees. If that wasn't enough, it rained most of that week, putting a real damper on any fun in the sun.

The kids kept begging me to go to Higgins, but I was determined not to. As we were returning home, the kids were in the back sleeping and I came to where the road from Mio intersects with Old US-76. If I turned left, I was heading home, and if I turned right, I headed up to Roscommon. I surprised the kids and made the detour to give them some time at the beach. When they woke up and noticed the familiar landmarks leading to a fun spot, they got so excited. I told them, "We are not going to the 'Peter-Pat' ranch [as they called it], but just to the beach."

Well, we got to the beach, and the rain moved in. Dena made lunch and made some boiled coffee to take the chill from of us. The three-foot whitecaps doused the thought of even getting wet, so we ate lunch and were getting ready to leave when Pat and Pete came driving into the park. Why? Why on earth would they be there on such a bad day? The park was several miles from their cottage.

They were as surprised as we were, and Pat said, "God must have sent you." We told her that we deliberately did not want to visit them because Pastor was getting some well-needed rest. She said, "Mom went home, and Pete had to go back on business, and I would be left without a car."

Pete was in the used-car business and had purchased several panel vans that came from RCA Victor and still had their advertising on them. He horse-traded one of them with a local for his business.

Pete asked for me to go with him to see what I thought of a parcel of land the buyer had for trade. I looked at a three-acre plot on a deeply rutted dirt road, which was overgrown with thicket, brush, and jack pines. It looked pretty rough to me, but then again, it was the deal.

Long story short, Pat and Pete thought Dena and I could use it to build our own getaway for us and our family. The next day he transferred the ownership to Dena and me, thus began our time of work, joy, relaxation, and family bonding.

I came into church the next Sunday, and a man said, "I hear you've got a piece of land." He kind of caught me off guard. He asked if I had wood I needed. When I indicated I did not, he offered me a two-and-a-half-car garage for the taking down of it. My sons and I took down every stick of siding and lumber and then pulled all the nails.

We hauled it up on a trailer, which took about twelve hours. The hardest part of the trip was through the West Branch hills. Back then there was no I-75, just a two-lane blacktop highway.

I had told Pete my plans to start with a garage-sized cabin, and the next time I saw Pete, he said, "You can start building, the slab is poured." I said, "Where?" and he responded, "Where you had the lumber off-loaded."

Then the real work began, and over all the years it never seemed to end. We built, built, built, and built. There was framing, electrical, plumbing, masonry, roofing, and so much more, but it was all a labor of love.

Our family bonded over those years by sharing times of work, sprinkled with times of fun.

Materials were never expensive, except the cost of the aspirin and Ben-Gay. For years our shower was Higgins Lake with a bar of soap. I'm sure we left a ring from time to time.

In the beginning the one-room cabin had two beds of steel box springs supported by cement blocks. Privacy was by using large sheets of material, supported by wire, much like a three-ring circus. There was one time early on when lack of beds put Jimmy on a salvaged door, on a cement washtub. The air mattress leaked, and by morning the doorknob left an indelible impression on his back.

As is on all construction sites, a porta-potty is very handy. Back then you couldn't rent them, and we were too busy to build one, so we propped a green door between two trees. The door had a window, so curtains were ordered, but delivery wouldn't happen until the next trip.

The future outhouse was made from several wooden old garage doors. Since this cabin was mainly for summer use, I used whatever materials I could scrounge. The windows were not insulated, and the size was dependent on what was available. I mounted aluminum storms on both the inside and outside. They kept the rain and snow out, but inside temperature usually matched the outside.

We seemed to always be expanding, expanding, and expanding, and for years it was just a tar-paper shack with wood slats holding the paper in place. In time I had Dena and the kids go up and down the roadsides to gather rocks to provide a stone-front base for aluminum siding. I was able to salvage some white siding, which I used in the back, which was less visible.

It may sound like all we did was work, not so! We found and cleaned out many a fishing hole. At times we would come back with enough fish to keep us cleaning them to wee hours of the morning.

When we first started on our endeavor, a friend came up to me and said, "Guess we won't see you much at church anymore since you have the cottage." He just didn't know us very well.

When we first started up there, a neighbor lady asked for us to come to a neighborhood barbecue. We went, and she asked us to pray over the meal. The Lord showed Dena and me that this depressed and poor area needed what God have given to us, and we quickly organized a Sunday school to be held in our place whenever we came up. Sunday mornings were special. Some of the kids came on bikes, some on horseback, some not so tidy, some without shoes, but all with a hunger to hear the Lord's Word. I would play my guitar or harmonica, and Dena would lead in songs, followed by scripture and a life lesson, and all kids left with a homemade treat.

At times we had twenty-five kids at our Sunday school in the Woods. One day, many years later, Dena and I were at Big Boy's in Grayling, and a young lady came up to us and said, "You're Mr. Dikin, aren't you?" I looked and did not recognize her. Then she said, "You taught me at your Sunday school many years ago, and now I am a Sunday school teacher." You know, you often wonder if you have planted the seed at the right time and at the right place… God never fails!

One vision that the Lord gave me was to have a small chapel at the end of our lane with a sign saying, "As You're on Your Way…Stop and Pray." It would have been unattended, just a place for all seeking God's provision, help, comfort, and peace and to bend their knee in private and connect with His mercy.

That vision could not be fulfilled by me. The Old US-76 highway is now replaced by I-75. But then, maybe the vision's time had not yet come. As we see the world around us getting more and more violent and pressures of life affecting all our families, maybe God is moving on another to do His bidding.

Well, because strain of age has come upon us, we had to sell the summer homestead, but our memories are as fresh as if it were yesterday.

The Spring of My Life

Even as the ground thaws after a long, very cold winter, so is the heart of man. Man goes through the times of life in cycles, much like the course of nature. The frozen ground warms ever so slowly, it seems. The surface cracks and swells, and soon a bud of green pushes its way to the surface above; the growth beneath the ground has begun long before it is ever visible. It is almost like the budding seed was yearning to see the sun in its fullness and is striving to bask in its glory.

The spiritual growth of man is very similar. A seed is planted deep within. Many think a farmer or gardener must plant the seed. Well, as that is true to a point, but many seeds are a result of past works of God and past gardeners. Several years back, I planted a little garden plot behind my shoe shop. It wasn't much of a garden, only a few plants. That year I didn't have the time to properly tend the garden, but it still yielded a crop. Many of the cherry tomatoes dropped off the vines and lay on the ground, a tribute to my intendedness. It was an embarrassment to acknowledge the ownership of a garden patch that was so neglected. Weeds obscured my perfectly set rows, as if to scoff my good intentions. Yet there was growth of the vine and fruit. God was faithful.

So is the life of man. The seed is planted. The Bible tells how the world's best Gardener explained the sower and the seed. Some seeds fell on stony and rocky soil; some among thorns and thistles; and some on well-prepared, good, rich soil. The planting of spiritual seed is much the same. Some hearts are tender, receptive, and rototilled by the one True Gardener. Not has only the surface of the soil been scratched, but the cultivation of the harrow and tiller has gone deep within. The seed is then planted. God can plant the seed; after all He is the Great Gardner. But then ofttimes He uses others to tend His garden. Remember, He may delegate various duties, such as planting, feeding, weeding, and keeping the birds and varmints from steeling the crop, but He does the preparation of the heart and waters the soul. I mentioned feeding, well, any good Gardener will praise the benefits of using manure to fertilize your crop. As I see it, the manure of life has given strength to my stalk and keeps my fruit from dropping from the vine before it is ready to be picked.

There was a time I hadn't planted a garden for a couple of years, but for those years God planted one for me. He took the seed I once planted and allowed it to sow itself time and again. Although we all go through the winters of life, our hope for tomorrow is that with the new day will come another thaw and a bursting forth of that seed God planted in each and every one of us. The rains will come. Some will be gully-washers, and some will be a subtle light sprinkle. Then comes the manure; remember, when it's being applied, it may be a time of disdain, and really stink, but it will help you to grow.

As you bud and blossom, and your fruit grows, share it with others. Sure, some isn't going to be picked and might fall to the ground, but God gives hope for another harvest.

Just believe!

He's My Best Friend
(Song to the Celtic tune "Oh, Danny Boy")

I have a friend in Whom I am confiding,
His presence fills my soul with joy each day.
A friend in Whom I have a peace abiding,
Ought can my heart with fear or dread dismay.
Come days of gloom with heavy weight of
sorrow,
Midst shadows deep temptations sharp and
keen.
This Friend so near, today, and through
tomorrow,
Dispells all fear, He ever stands between.
This Friend of mine is Christ the Rock of Ages,
I will trust Him while here on earth I roam.
He'll keep me safe though storm of life rages,
Till comes the morn within my heavenly
home.
Refrain:
He's my Best Friend, to Him my soul is
clinging,
My Rock, my Strength, in every hour of need.
While He is near, my heart is ever singing,
I have a Friend, Who is a friend indeed.

Note:

This was the cobbler's favorite song. I cannot find these lyrics elsewhere, so he may have penned them himself, or adopted them, but I know they were in his heart continually.

A Home Is Not a Home without a Lot of Work

When Dena and I first got married, we rented an upper flat on Van Dyke, in Warren Township, Michigan. At that time, we embarked on starting our family, and on May 20, 1935, our first child was born. Dena Mae was our pride and joy, and we were so happy that God blessed us with her.

We had chosen that flat because the rent was something we could afford at the time. Our stay there was riddled with problems; most of which was trying to keep warm. The landlord lived downstairs, and when he went off to work, he would turn down the heat to reduce costs. We had no control of the temperature and were often left cold. Having a baby in this type of environment was causing us much concern, especially as she developed bad colds, which led to pneumonia. Back then, doctors were hard to find, and if you found one close enough, you couldn't afford the visit. Home remedies were relied on, and in Dena Mae's case, they did not improve her health. We lost our baby on January 18, 1936.

Dena and I were so broken with this loss. It took a while to take hold of reality, and we started to look for another place to live. Dena said, "Raleigh, I'm a city girl, and I do not want to live in the country." Well, we looked all over, and the homes we loved were way out of our price range. So we slowly kept heading further and further away from the Detroit city limits. One mile out, on a dirt road called Piper Boulevard, we passed a small, somewhat-dilapidated, asbestos-sided bungalow. I drove past it, and Dena said, "Raleigh, Raleigh, stop!" I looked and saw the wood planks as a makeshift sidewalk and an outhouse behind this seemingly wreck of a house, but there was a "for sale" sign in front. Reluctantly I stopped. We checked it out, and she said, "We can make this work," although I had my doubts. Not only that, but could I actually make something out of this eyesore?

We found that the price was $700 plus a couple hundred in back taxes. That was workable, but was it worth it? I would say so. The land included an adjacent vacant corner lot, which was probably the best part of the deal.

The house was a one-story with kitchen and two bedrooms. I guess they would call it a "starter home"—that is not what I called it, but Dena said, "I can make us a nice home here," so we closed the deal and started working on our dream home.

The house was tilting due to rotted cedar piers, so I decided to raise it up, dig new footings, and install new block piers. I got to work. I used borrowed bottle jacks and raised it up to work in the crawl space. I dug out the footings and acquired the blocks for piers. All was going well… Then it rained…and rained… and rained. My eighteen-inch holes became flooded and widened to two and a half foot each. And if that wasn't bad enough, the house slipped northward to the neighbor's property. I was back to square one. I finally got it back to where it belonged, redid the footings with wooden forms, and poured the cement foundations, then laid the permanent block piers.

Every waking moment, I was working to make our forever home more livable. I expanded in each direction, resulting in a house with an upstairs, four bedrooms, large kitchen, one and a half baths, utility room, second-story addition, den, family room, and an attached garage. It seems the thirty-six years we lived at the homestead, we were always in project mode. I was so happy that as time progressed, Dena and I had three boys, who grew up quickly as they helped me do the various home improvements. Everything took money and time, so I had to take on extra side jobs to get funds for the materials. The other concern was the time it took to see improvement results.

There was always something to do. The original heating system I installed was hydronic with a coal-fired boiler and radiators (later baseboard heat).

I remember my brother John had some live ducks for us to butcher and eat. We weren't home, so he just dropped them into the coal chute. When I got home and read the note he left me, I went down to check out our newly delivered dinners. They were four foul fowls. They were so covered with soot I had to use Ivory soap to wash them after I plucked their feathers. But they were free, and they tasted pretty good.

The boiler was later converted to natural gas when it became available in the neighborhood. Besides the normal painting, I rewired, replumbed, made new kitchen cabinets, reroofed, fenced the total property, built ceramic tables and china wall cabinets.

I couldn't afford contractors, so I did the work myself (with my boys).

We enjoyed barbecues, and I made two different ones out of brick. I built one beauty, only to have to demolish it when I built the family room between the back of the house and the garage.

Years later, I did have a contractor build my two-and-a-half-car block garage on the rear of the corner lot for my new shoe shop. I had been using the garage attached to the house, but I needed a freestanding building if I was to build my business.

As I installed bathroom facilities, and since sewer service was not yet available, I made a homemade concrete septic tank, and I added a front porch of concrete and bricks. Whenever I did concrete work, I would use that opportunity to dispose of all my salvage scrap steel and iron. I buried it as reinforcement to the concrete.

After thirty-six years at the house on MacArthur (formerly Piper Boulevard), the local school board decided they needed our homestead to expand their parking lot for the high school. We were heartbroken. After many negotiations and the following court case decision, we accepted the inevitable. We had to move on, but I had the last laugh. Remember that extra steel I put into the front porch and septic tanks? I sat in my car and watched them demolish my house, my work of art, with tears in my eyes; those tears of sorrow became tears of laughter. The guy on this large dozer took a running start toward the porch, and as he hit it, the dozer stopped, and the operator, not so much. He almost left the cab due to the abrupt stop. The porch and tank were solid and would not move easily.

With the funds from the school board settlement for our home and corner-lot business, God provided enough for a beautiful custom brick home in the seven-mile outer drive area, and we lived there many years until it was time to downsize. Our new home had a large living room with fireplace, three bedrooms, large kitchen, Florida room, and fully finished basement and two-and-a-half-car brick garage. There were also fruit trees and plenty of garden space. Our new house was like a mansion compared to our old homestead.

The Thanksgiving

One of the spiritual milestones in my life began with my employment at the US Rubber Company, the predecessor of Uniroyal. Throughout life there were times which tested my courage and my faith in God. The daily challenges in a world so filthy and corrupt will either taint your life or make you a stronger Christian.

Being a supplier of products needed for the war effort, US Rubber provided a safe haven for me, and I was exempted from the draft. Dena and I had four children at the time, and being able to serve my country here at home was a blessing. Little did I know, my faith and courage would be tested in a way I never expected.

I had worked several positions as pressman, running stock through hot, noisy presses in an environment and under conditions that modern-day OSHA would love to shut down. This was at a time when labor unions were young and did not have the voice or respect they enjoy today. Temperatures exceeded 120 degrees, and the dust and fumes from the rubber and solvents made the job not only hazardous but also at times downright impossible.

I had attended a union meeting in a smoke-filled hall with a couple hundred workers where I witnessed the vulgarity and open display of infidelity as married men were pursuing female workers openly. There was almost a carnival atmosphere, and the workers seemed to be in one accord in their hatred of the company they worked for. I was taught to respect those who are over you, to live peaceably and honorably. I sat back and listened and watched until I had enough... You see, soon they started singing a song which seemed familiar to me. It was to the tune of "The Old Rugged Cross," but these men desecrated it by singing "The Old Rotten Boss." I had enough of this... I left.

I wouldn't pay my union dues because I couldn't. Not because of the money, but because to support an organization so strongly opposed to peace and God was repulsive to me. Finally, my boss called me in and explained that I either had to join the union and pay the dues or they would have to let me go. I conceded but told them, "I will pay my dues, but I will curse each dollar, and it will not benefit the union." That seemed to be an acceptable position to them.

As I kept working, I gained favor with management. I guess they saw I had developed skills and job knowledge, and when they needed a supervisor, they called me into the office. When the position was offered to me, I told the superintendent that I didn't think I could do the job since I only had an eighth-grade education and no prior supervisory experience. He said, "I heard you are a Sunday school teacher, and if you can teach children, you will be able to teach and lead men." What could I say? I accepted the promotion.

Little did I know, but soon my time with US Rubber would soon be over.

I was working the night shift, and one night one of my workers came in with liquor on his breath. I took him aside and told him he would have to go home, that I couldn't let him operate presses in his intoxicated condition. He begged me not to send him home since he would lose a day's pay and leave a bad mark on his work record. I told him I would watch him and if his safety or that of his coworkers was threatened, I would send him home.

I went back to running my press, and soon I didn't see that worker anymore until the end of the shift. When he returned, he ran some production, but it was all undercured and scrap. He also had taken all the stock I ran that night and rubbed off my identifying code and replaced it with his own. When I saw the scrap that he ran and what he did to cover up his production loss, I confronted him. He picked up a steel bar and threatened to kill me. I reported the incident to the superintendent and did not go to work for the next three days.

My boss stopped by the house on the third day and asked me to return to work for a meeting to review the situation. When I entered his office, there was the worker that threatened me, the foremen, union officials, and the big boss. I was told I had the support of management to prosecute the worker, but instead I offered him my hand to him. I said, "I tried to protect you, and you chose to threaten me. I forgive you, please don't let it happen again." After that meeting, I asked my boss for a thirty-day leave of absence, which he granted me.

During my time off, I worked around the house and repaired shoes in my little shoe shop in the garage. After the thirty days were up, I still wasn't up to returning to my old job, and I asked for an extension of the leave, which my boss rejected. After eleven years with the company, I felt it was time to move on, and with Dena's support, I quit my job.

My faith in God was strong, and in my heart I knew He would never let me down. As time went on, I busied myself with work around the house, and the income from shoe repairing was about fifteen dollars per week. We were entering that time where they say you must "fish…or cut bait." I couldn't fish (I had no money for the bait). I couldn't cut bait because my knives were dull. Dena could always make something to eat from seemingly very little, but now the cupboards were bare. And then there was tomorrow, *Thanksgiving Day.*

Did I miss God? Some would say an emphatic "*Yes.*" I thought that God in His infinite mercy and grace surely wouldn't let my family suffer. I knew when I left my job it was the right decision, but now I was hurt, confused, and although the family was strong and understanding during this time, how could I face tomorrow?

The best thing to do when you think you might have missed the boat is to call out to the Skipper. That's what I did! I needed to find a place where I could be alone, so I climbed to the attic of the garage. The attic had become a place of dust, spiders, mice, and old discarded items, but that day it became my prayer closet.

The scripture tells us that when you pray and the burden is so heavy that you don't know how to pray, the Holy Spirit prays through you in groaning and words which express your innermost needs to your Heavenly Father. That day I met God in such a way I cannot fully express in words. I don't remember all I prayed, but I do remember what was important. My prayer time ended with me asking God, "What am I going to do about tomorrow—it being Thanksgiving?" He said, "Be thankful for that which you have!" I responded, "Lord, Dena has made meal after meal with seemingly nothing to make it with, and if I had a loaf of bread, I wouldn't ask you for another…but, Lord, we have nothing." As I knelt the broken and humble, God said, "You have Me!"

At that point I felt the whole world was lifted from my shoulders, and I wiped the tears from my eyes and left my prayer room to face the world in the strength of His power.

As I came out of the garage, a neighbor lady was coming up the walk with sacks of groceries in her arms. She was of a different faith, but what she did and when she did it tells me she was God's way of proving to me that I *had Him*!

That Thanksgiving Day was not only a day of thanks but also a day of new beginnings. The next day the treasurer from the church we were attending called to ask if I would clean the church for Sunday, since their cleaning lady had quit. That Sunday I was told the pastor was very happy with the work I did, and the church offered me a full-time job, which I retired from some thirty-two years later.

Postscript

Aurel Dikin Sr. started teaching Sunday school in the coal room of the basement church (after cleaning each week) and continued to teach Sunday school for many years, and wife Dena (who was a teen evangelist before they married) taught thousands of kids and adults over a thirty-year period.

They even had a Sunday school on Milliken Lane for many years and touched many young lives when they came North to rest on weekends.

Mom and Dad passed away years ago, and I promised them I would share their stories with others.

Opportunity Knocks

THE STORY OF THE GOOD SAMARITAN

I expect to pass through this world only once, any good thing therefore that I can do, or any kindness that I can show to any fellow creature, let me do it now, let me not defer or neglect it, for I shall not pass this way again. (Stephen Grellet)

This poem I had found in a frame, and its message and meaning rang true to me personally. I mounted it to the inside door of my janitor's room, where it remained until the day I retired. *God is good, always!*

New Shoes for Easter

This memory is of a simpler time, when people worked hard to make every effort to earn income in whatever legal way possible to meet their daily needs. There was never time or money to buy things we wanted, but God always provided for our needs, but we did have to work for them.

I picked up so many "side jobs" to supplement the meager salary I received as a custodian of a large church. My sons and I would cut down trees, tear down and remove nails on old garages to save the wood, tile basement floors, do odd plumbing and electric jobs, etc. Besides all this, I also had a shoe shop next to our house.

Dena would take in, tag the repair needed, and after I had performed my magic, would release the repaired shoes. You see, I had learned from my dad how to apply his can-do skills to make new-like shoes out of ratty and stinky old ones. Shoemaking is an art form. Pa learned how to make shoes by hand in Romania as a young man. He would make a pattern of the client's foot out of newspaper. He then selected the proper leather, hand-cut the materials and even made his own thread out of flax. He would spin it on his leg and wax it with bee's wax. He used an awl to make the holes in the new sole and welt (the strip glued to the top of the shoe or boot). He would then trim any access materials and used cut glass to finish the edge, followed by using a hot wax candle to "burnish" it to a prime finish after applying the stain.

Following Pa's lead, I assisted him in his shoe shops on Van Dyke in Detroit. At a point in time, I opened my own shop in the frame garage to the rear of our house. As my "business" grew, I had a cement block garage built on the corner of McArthur and Dodge Street in Warren, Michigan. The house we had was on the same corner property, and it seemed to be an ideal situation. In time, Pa and I acquired power equipment that greatly improved the work quality and shortened the repair time.

I guess it was in about 1954, and it was the night before Easter. I had finished all the customer's shoes and had Jimmy bring the family's shoes to the shop for Easter dress-up. There were eight of us, three boys, three girls, and Dena and I. Jimmy brought all the Easter footies out to me, and I began my magic. Later that night when I was finished, I had put all the family's completed shoes in a brown paper bag and Jimmy was to take them into the house. This was where everything started to go haywire.

Jimmy, at the age of ten, was so excited to come into the house and see my wife and several of the other kids at the large kitchen table coloring eggs for the next day. They were having fun, and he felt somewhat left out having to play gopher. He set the bag at the side of the kitchen near the radiator and jumped in to getting his hands stained like the others.

All was joyous, and they had a ball until bedtime. Easter morning was normal…a great breakfast (they were always great meals—just look at us). Everybody was getting dressed, and then came the dilemma… Where are the shoes?

I asked Jimmy, "Where is that sack of shoes I sent in with you?" He said, "Right over there," and pointed by the kitchen wall. Oops, the bag he was pointing to was the trash bag. I came in from my shop late the night before and had grabbed the "bag of trash" and took it out to the backyard burn barrel.

When I surmised what could have happened, I hightailed it to the burn barrel, just to find a smoldering pile of partial soles and heels. The whole family's shoes were gone. Nowadays, some would find this situation reason enough to stay home from church… Not me, not today. I took the phone book and found the home number of Bill Romano, who owned a shoe store on Van Dyke and Nine Mile. I knew Mr. Romano as an acquaintance, but we were not good friends at that time. You see, a cobbler fixes worn shoes so people don't have to buy new ones. I told Bill the story, and Bill said, "Meet me at the store right away, and I'll get you what you need." I told him I didn't have money to buy them, but if he would help us, I would pay him the next week when I got paid.

Well, all ended fine. We all got new shoes, I picked up a few side jobs to meet my obligation, and I'm sure the Lord's direction on Mr. Romano's life might have had something to do with him becoming a state representative, then state senator.

The following bio is from the State of Michigan House of Representatives:

> **Romano, William (1911–1966)**—of Van Dyke (now part of Warren), Macomb County, Mich. Born in Cherokee, Crawford County, Kan., January 22, 1911. Married, November 27, 1937, to Angela Tranchida. Democrat. Deputy sheriff; police chief; restaurant business; shoe merchant; member of Michigan state house of representatives, 1945-64 (Macomb County 2nd District 1945-54, Macomb County 1st District 1955-64); member of Michigan state senate 27th District, 1965–66. Catholic. Member, Knights of Columbus; Eagles. At the scene of a hotel fire, he lifted up a heavy fire hose which had pinned a woman to a car; then suffered a fatal heart attack, 1966 (age about 55 years). Burial location unknown.

The two father and son cobblers are center and right

Let's Go Fishing

Fishing… It is said that true fishing is a piece of line with a jerk on each end. Well, I resemble that, and I'm proud to say it! You may think this isn't a fair assessment of my condition, but I'm incurable when it comes to my love for my fin-feathered friends.

To me, fishing is much more than what you catch, although I do love the taste of freshly caught vitals. Fishing is my way to unwind, kick back, and enjoy the only contact sport that provides proof to your wife that you were really doing what you said you were doing. The cologne you wear on your clothes and the worm residue under your fingernails tells a story of how your day went onboard your dingy.

Let's not get ahead of the story… I didn't always have my own boat. I would rent boats wherever the time and finances led me. I would fish from the dock when I couldn't afford to "go aboard" and was just as satisfied. Fishing was my connection with my "Maker." Many an hour I would meditate, contemplate, and pray while watching for the bounce of my bobber. For those who are not tuned into the fisherman's lingo, a bobber is a device that gives you a visual connection with what is happening under the surface of the water. It can be any shape, any color, and made of anything that floats. My favorite is the two-toned, red-and-white, round plastic ones. It seemed to be Dena's favorite as well and also my kids', so much so that I had to put "AD" on all mine to keep my tackle box from becoming an empty box. You lose a lot of tackle over the years, especially bobbers. When they started importing the ones I love from China, I found the quality sincerely lacking. They would break easily as you bounce them off a log, or the springlike gizmo that held unto your line would malfunction and your bobber would either sink or swim. Bobber pollution is a major environmental concern, and I believe we can blame it on the imported ones.

Sinkers, on the other hand, are my friends. They come in all sizes and shapes, but the color is always gunmetal gray. I have a never-ending supply since I make my own. I have molds and find it to be a relaxing hobby to create useful trinkets from scrap molten lead. I would pick up the lead from discarded wheel balancing shims, and now and then I would come across a lead bonanza. I remember this one time a friend of mine had an x-ray machine sales and repair facility. Sammy said that lead was used as counterbalance for the tip-up table mechanism on these medical units. He was scrapping one, and the three-inch, pipe-shaped lead logs created sinkers for all my needs and those of all my fishing friends and relatives. The EPA never got wind of the lead I was smelting, and since my mind and body weren't affected by the exposure to this supposed pollutant, maybe it's not that bad, or maybe God was watching over His "fishing buddy."

Fishing sometimes provides unexpected treasures. Sometimes you hook unto a prize lure or setup someone else lost. Sometimes it's a discarded boot or tire. But then sometimes it's fodder for real storytelling.

My Arms Are Tired, and My Sunburn Hurts

One day I decided to go fishing on the Detroit River. I drove to the foot of Alter Road and Jefferson, rented a flat-bottom wooden boat, and put out for a daylong adventure. Little did I know what "daylong" really meant. With no motor, I rowed upstream so that when I was finished, I could drift back to my departure area, thus making it easy at the end of day. Over the hours, I caught a few, and since it was cloudy, I was very comfortable in my shorts. Little did I realize that the UV rays penetrate through the clouds, and as I was ready to pull up anchor and drift, I noticed I was taking on a slight pink tone on my overexposed long legs.

Unconcerned at the time, I "weighed anchor." It seemed to weigh enough. It was one of your normal rental anchors, a large coffee can with an eyebolt filled with cement. There was no wind, and the current seemed not to be helping me attain my downstream goal. So I rowed and rowed and rowed. Never before did I have so much trouble controlling a rowboat, and my easy return took an hour or so longer than I had expected. Then there was my developing sunburn… I really wanted this ordeal to end, and end quickly, but the torment continued.

When I finally pulled into the rental dock and the owner came out to check me back in, I had to tell him there was something wrong with this boat. I explained not being able to control it and how hard it was to row. He couldn't understand. He looked, and the anchor was sitting there on the floor… Then he said, "What's that rope over the gunnels?" I had never noticed it before. And when I pulled it up, I found that my anchor had somehow grabbed hold of another with a long anchor rope still attached and I had been dredging the river for hours without knowing.

It was a beautiful anchor. It wasn't your normal rental make-do type but a nice swing shaft anchor that looked like a miniature of those I saw on the freighters that passed (and almost swamped me) on the river. The owner offered to buy the anchor from me. I refused! This was my treasure, and I still have this memento I worked for so hard.

A Tackle Box Full, but All I Need Is Crawlers

Over the years I've been schmoozed, tempted, and often gave into temptations to buy the latest and most promising gimmicks which claim to "lure" the lunkers to my line. Amid the newest fad always came the disclaimer that "sometimes no matter what you offer, the fish are just not biting." And if they don't bite, you can't catch them, so why spend a lot of money on things that have limits to your fishionary success? As for me, and my house, we will use worms. Usually, bigger is better, but if using crawlers, we use the "pinch a piece" policy. Never use a full crawler if a piece will do. The downside to live bait is that you can run out just when the fishing goes hot and heavy. But if you do, you can pull out the rubber worm backup plan. You may notice by now that I'm more for putting meat on the table than a trophy on the wall. Give me a mess of sweet-tasting pan fish any day over their Goliath-sized cousins, although getting a big one now and then gives certain bragging rights.

Crawlers… You can buy them, sure, but that's not much fun. Years ago, I started harvesting my own from my lawn. The day before my fishing trip, I would cut the grass, then after sunset I would water the lawn for about an hour. I made my "lightning rod" from a scrap wooden handled weed whip. I cut off the L-shaped whip end and ground the rod tip to a point. I then wired it by taping *one* lead of an extension cord to the rod near the grip and isolated the other wire by taping it, making it "dead." After prepping the grass, I would then grab my flashlight, plug in my lightning rod, and push my probe into the lawn, beginning my treasure hunt. You must walk softly and not carry your big stick. The rod, with the moistened ground, creates a force field that is intolerable to the unsuspecting crawlers. They are sensitive to light, but by moving stealthily and quickly, you can get a few dozen in an hour or so. The rod produces a vibration to the soil, and the crawlers seek the surface quickly. I'm sure OSHA would not approve of my tool, but I won't tell them if you don't. Wear rubber boots to keep your feet dry and provide insolating properties for your safety.

Let's Go Home… This Place Is Starting to Stink!

There was a small group of like-minded anglers from our church that planned a fishing trip to our neighbors to the North, in Canada. There was a place on the Trent River that was a hiding spot for lunkers. I was invited to join since they knew I had an inside track to dropping hooks, and I was a pretty good camp cook. This "resort" was just a group of simple cabins in a line overlooking this picturesque river. A manually operated lock system controlled the level of this floodwater area while allowing river traffic to transverse up and downstream. It operated the same way the Panama Canal connects the Atlantic and Pacific oceans through Central America. The camp was at Peterborough, Ontario, Canada (northeast of Toronto).

The week was quite an adventure. With the cabin came a couple of boats with motors, and we caught fish—boy, did we catch fish! Each evening we would spend time cleaning them and putting them in the freezer to be taken back home as a treat for our wives and families. I don't remember the limits (if there were any), but when we came home, we had wooden crates packed with sawdust with the larger of our frozen treasures kept solid for the trip back to the States. Each night we had a fish fry; by the end of the week, I was again longing for some of Dena's home cooking. Don't get me wrong—I love fish, but you can overdo a good thing.

I remember this one day, we were out on the river, and I was looking for my rosary. This not being disrespectful to my Catholic friends, but that is what I called my red-beaded, three-hook night crawler harness. I knew I bought one, and I knew I had seen it earlier that day; I just couldn't find it. I just kept using my old harness, and at the end of day, when I was getting out of the sloop, I found it. *Ouch*! I was sitting on it, and it had connected itself with one hook to my boat cushion and another hook to my bottom. I wasn't sure if I was laughing or crying…probably a little of both! My fishing buddy helped me get unstuck, and then the laughing really started. You've got to realize…a fish hook has barbs meant to keep them from being spit out by the fish. Well, that was not working in my favor. That night I stood around a lot, while the others were kicking back and relaxing.

Well, as all good things must come to an end, so did this beautiful week on the Trent River. Pop Baer announced our need to return to civilization with a "We gotta get out of here, it's starting to stink." I suppose it wouldn't have been so bad if we weren't so successful, but there is always a downside to having a good time, and our maid wasn't brought on this trip.

Most men, when they leave on a trip, they bring their loved ones a small memento to reward those who had to stay home. We brought home boxes of frozen fish packed in sawdust. Oh well!

At a later date I took the family to the same camp as a family vacation, and my oldest son, Richard, helped turn the manual turn style to level the locks as the queen's royal cruiser was allowed passage. Later Jimmy got married, and he took his wife and in-laws up there for a vacation. I understand the river is still there, and "the water runs through it."

Take a Boy Fishing Today

The job I had for over thirty-two years required me to work half days on Saturday each and every week. As head of maintenance for a very large church, it was my responsibility to prepare all areas for the day ahead. To compensate me for this weekend commitment, I was given the full day off on Tuesdays. That was my day to catch up around the house and, on occasion, go fishing with either Pa or my brother-in-law Bob. These times were rare, but we would find a lake with a boat rental and spend the day drowning worms. We would bring home our catch and prep them for the cooks.

One Monday evening, I started putting together my tackle for one of those Tuesday getaways. I planned to take Pa out on Orchard Lake for some quality time. Jimmy saw what I was doing and asked if he could be a tagalong. He was about ten at the time, and since *he* didn't have Tuesdays off from school, I had to give him the bad news. He walked away saddened, but rules were rules.

The next morning Dena was busy making breakfast, and as I took my place at the table, I saw something on my plate I didn't expect. Jimmy had gone to my tackle box and put a small tin container on my dish. It was a split shot box, and on it was the message, "Take a boy fishing today." Something tugged at my heart, and I couldn't deny such a noble and sincere request. I hugged him and told him to grab his rod.

I'm a firm believer in rules, and for the most part, consistency is important, but also more importantly is the bond that connects father and son. We found our time together to be good times, whether working or playing.

Fishing at the Cottage

Over fifty years ago, and to coincide with starting our Northern Michigan adventure building a summer cottage, we found through our neighbor Harry Bowman that there was a river that flowed from Houghton Lake all the way to Lake Michigan. We found that the floodwaters created from dams on the river produced areas looking like the Florida Everglades. This is terrific habitat for all types of fowl, fish, deer, bear, and all other creatures. Being a floodwater area, the river channel cuts through the marshland and the fishing possibilities abound. With all the hidden stumps, you rarely find boaters unless they are fishing, canoeing, hunting, or studying nature. The seclusion is a safe haven for those seeking solace. There are beavers, otters, ospreys, and bald eagles as well as fishing for the adventurous. I once saw a bald eagle swoop down, hook about a twelve-inch bass swimming too close to the surface and, with its talons took it up into a tree nest overlooking the river to feed its family.

Back in the fifties and early sixties, there was a sincere effort to study and later ban the use of DDT, a widely used farming insecticide. It was found that the bald eagle was bordering on extinction, and DDT was the expected culprit. The chemical was contaminating the water and food source of the eagles and resulted in their eggshells being too weak to withstand normal wild incubation.

One day, back in the wilds, at the edge of the river, we found a small contingent of men on a mission. They had a converted school bus for housing and two boat-type vehicles. They worked for a philanthropist and were to find nests, take the eggs, and place them in a portable incubator to transport them to a university for safe hatching. I looked over the equipment these guys had. There was what they called their "stump jumper," which looked much like a pontoon boat, except the pontoons had spiral fins attached and rotated separately so they could power and steer it by stopping or reversing one or the other. The boat's operation was neat, and they could walk over the stumps, allowing them to maneuver close to the nests. This boat was powered by a V-8 Buick engine, and its H-type construction allowed it to get right up to the tree being searched. There was a tall "A-frame" ladder attached, providing easy access to the heights needed. The other boat was a "jet-powered" boat, the first I had ever seen. The sponsor of this expedition was providing a serious approach to this operation, and over the years we have seen his efforts rewarded by the bald eagles' return to comfortable levels.

The river has held our favor for over fifty years, and three generations still call it our "go-to" location for meat. Bluegill, northern pike, bass (both big-mouth and small-mouth), rock bass, crappie, perch, catfish, and the massive dogfish visit our lines. In the evening hours, and for night fishing, there are the bullheads and catfish. The grandkids always chuckle when I'm cleaning bullheads because I tell them I had to "pull off their pajamas" when I skin them.

My cottage fishing mentor, Harry, was an interesting man. He was a chain-smoker, and he would saddle the cigarette between his index and middle finger and kept his hand in place while he smoked almost like he was holding his nose. But Harry knew where to fish and what to use. He'd use lures, but none of them were the shiny ones like I had in my fine tackle box. His were old and rusted. His tackle box was an old, five-gallon plastic bucket with a dozen or so daredevils in various sizes, although their color was hard to determine. His rods were nothing special, but they did the job. Rarely did he get skunked, and I learned much about the sport of fishing from a "local."

My Wife and Daughter Have a Surprise for Me

One day Dena and her chauffer, my daughter Myrtle, went shopping. They stopped by Sears and saw that they had aluminum fishing boats on sale. They picked out a fourteen-foot, heavy-duty, wide-beam boat then came home to tell me to go pick it up.

To say the least, I was really surprised. I had a station wagon with a roof rack, so I went to pick up the family's most recent purchase. The metal was much better than many of the small boats I'd seen. When I passed it down to Jimmy, he told of a fishing day he was spending with his wife and kids, and for some reason a hole (probably from a bad rock he hit) sprang a leak, and water was spewing up like a fountain. His five-year-old daughter Wendy started screaming that they were goanna sink. Jimmy simply reached into his tackle box and brought out a Black Cow taffy sucker… He moistened some and plugged the hole. They all had a good laugh and passed around the rest of the sucker. You see, I taught him how to share. Later when they got home, he made a simple plug of a small bolt and nut with a rubber washer on the top and bottom. After all these years, and being passed down through the family, it's now my grandson Dave's, and he treasures his heirloom.

The Bear Truth

One Saturday afternoon, the boys decided to go to the gravel pit to do a little target practice. Hunting season was moving in on us, and they wanted to sight in their rifles. The girls said, "Don't be long…dinner will be ready soon." All was good. Jim's son Bobby took his new pickup truck, and they headed off to the pits. Bobby was bragging on his new purchase and went off-trail and soon buried his brand-new truck axle-deep in loose sand. Not being a four-by-four, Bob's new Ford was no match for the sand dune. They worked over an hour when, finally, some guys happened by to help get the truck unstuck.

The boys figured they were going to be on the receiving end of their wife's anger for such carelessness, so they developed a story. They told them that their delay was "because a big, black bear attacked them, and they had to hide and wait until it went away." It was a lame story, and everyone knew it!

After dinner we went fishing. Jim drove with Bob, and Mike with me in the back seat. When driving home (north on Old-27 just past the Muskegon River bridge), a black bear ran out of the woods right in front of the car. When we got back to the cottage, the guys told the girls what they saw.

Wendy said, "Yeah sure, I'll bet it was just a raccoon dragging a couple of garbage bags across the road."

The boys knew that the story, although true, would be questioned due to their shenanigans earlier. I told them…"I saw it too, and *I don't lie.*" This was probably God's way of letting the guys know that He's always watching!

The Making of a Boat Trailer

A had a friend who had a friend with some shoe repair machinery to get rid of. He was cleaning out *his* garage. This was a twelve-foot-long finishing machine. A finishing line has several different adapters for various grades of sandpaper and even edge cutters for shoe-repair finishing. I didn't really need a machine this big (it was a duplication of a finisher I already had), but I did need a boat trailer. The one-inch-and-a-half-diameter-long steel pipes would be perfect, and the large electric motor would be backup for my finisher. We wrestled the machine unto a trailer and hauled it across the city to become a "Rollo Dikin, one-of-a-kind creation." Little did we know how hard the pipe would be to cut with a hacksaw. This was way before the Sawzall or pneumatic cutoff blades. So for hours my sons and I took turns exercising our biceps. Ben-Gay provided relief for us as we healed from our sawing efforts. With the pipes all cut, I now searched for the remaining parts to complete the boat hauler I designed. I found an axle from a '49 Ford. That's good, right? Not so much. Although the axle came with wheels and tires, matching the lug pattern was difficult in finding a spare. I then found leaf springs and a hitch and hauled everything to a local welder and a week later we got our "dingy dolly." We drilled holes in the pipes and used eyebolts to secure a volume of old rubber washing machine wringer rollers. This trailer carried a fourteen-foot aluminum boat, ofttimes loaded with construction materials, to our upstate hideaway. I remember one day I asked Jimmy to load some salvaged cement blocks and bricks he had cleaned of mortar. I was at work and, being a Friday night, was in a hurry to get the family loaded up for our trek North. The boat was loaded…boy, was it loaded. Jimmy had lined the bottom with cement and cinder blocks and then inserted a brick in each web of each block. When I pointed out the flattened tires to him, we laughed a little, then he unloaded about half.

That trailer worked well for many years. There was only one problem I remember. My daughters had taken the boat North with a girlfriend and, returning late on a Sunday night, crossed a railroad track just east of Vassar. At a speed of about fifty miles per hour, the hitch snapped. The weight of the hitch-less pipe dug into the tracks, and the boat and trailer made a triple pirouette. Nothing came out of the boat. The boat cover kept everything inside, and the only damage was a slightly bent gunnel at the right oarlock. When telling this story, many would question its validity, but a state trooper that was directly behind had not only witnessed this, but also contacted a local mechanic who welded the hitch back on and put the girls back on the road in the middle of a Sunday night.

Go Fish!

I have a good friend that would have me and my sons go out on Lake St. Clair fishing. Al was a CPA and provided all his friends necessary services to get them through the IRS maze of rules and regulations during tax season. If Al was still around, he would be a strong competitor to H&R Block. Al was also a fellow elder in our church and had a dingy a little larger than mine. His first one was twenty-one feet, then his last was a twenty-five-foot cabin cruiser. Al would fill up with petro, and we would head out to his hot spot on Lake St. Clair. We would bottom-fish for perch, and he always had two rods going at the same time. Sitting on his captain's chair, he had one rod in each hand and would alternate an up-and-down yank to keep the bait moving. I just used one rod with two hooks and didn't use Al's up-down jerky motion, and I always brought home the "bacon"... Al, not so much.

I guess you'd consider me a serious fisherman. I've fished internationally on the Georgian Bay in Ontario and Port Peele for smelt. I've fished Lake Huron for perch on a charter boat, Lake St. Clair, the Detroit River, and many of the inland lakes in Oakland County.

If you want to clear your mind of your daily rituals and the confusion of a fast-paced world, leave your iPod, laptop, and cell phone behind, and grab your rod and tackle box and "take a boy fishing…today." The boy doesn't have to be *your* boy, maybe a neighbor's or friend's. The rewards will be endless for both you and him (or her)!

Greater Love

Greater love has no man than this, than to lay down one's life for his friends. (John 15:13)

The Greatest Love
(For my wife, Dena)

Is that a man would lay down his life for his wife, for she is his friend, his sweetheart, his wife, and mother of their children. (Aurel Dikin Sr.)

A Lullaby of Love
(by Aurel Dikin Sr.)

Refrain:

Rock me to sleep in that old rocking chair, Daddy

Rock me to sleep and sing a Southern Ayer, oh, Daddy,

Rock me to sleep, how I wish I were there,

Rocking in that old rocking chair.

I know when day is done, and with the setting sun,

The moon has risen high up in the sky.

I can almost see me there, in that old rocking chair,

As I'd climb upon his knee and he'd sing this song to me.

The Cobbler's Day Job(s)

As I look back at jobs I've had over the years, I am amazed and amused at the varied abilities that my Heavenly Father has entrusted to his humble servant.

A few years back, in the prime of my "growth spurt," I found that being the oldest in a family of twelve kids had responsibility that goes far beyond the title "firstborn." As a youth I would help Ma with the laundry. There was the fire building, hauling water, scrubbing, hanging, and taking down the family clothes. Since there wasn't much money, Ma made many of the clothes, and she insisted on us being clean and presentable. It was that "cleanliness/godliness" thing.

Growing up in farm country, there was always something to do. My dad was busy trying to earn enough to put bread on the table, so I had to grow up fast. Pa didn't drive, so as I reached the age of fourteen, I would drive him over the countryside and from state to state as he performed his duties as a fur and wool grader. Pa could tell where an animal was from and what type of food it ate by feeling the pelt. There were mink, fox, rabbit, badger, beaver, among others. He would then establish a fair price for the pelts, and we would be on our way to the next trapper's farm or shack. Bags of wool were tall and had to be packed to allow the volumes to be readied for shipment. We would jump into the open half-full bags to provide compression. Ticks and other insects would be part of our clothing and require removal. "Off" with Deet wasn't available, and we just lived with the discomfort. At times I would look like a five-year-old with chicken pox, but it was just scars from the bloodsucking pests.

Fuel for Thought

Sometimes Pa would work the night shift at other jobs, and I would have to drive him to town and then pick him up afterward. There was a time when we were living at the top of a hill, and one day with Pa at work and the car out of gas, I looked down the hill and saw the gas truck at the end of the drive. Boy, what luck. I pushed the car to the edge of the hill and jumped in. I was on my way…faster and faster, then as I got to the bottom and was going to stop right behind the truck. I had downshifted and was able to slow Ole Betsey down, but when I went to brake, it was the clutch I pushed. Oops! Right into the back end of the truck. There was quite a jolt, and the valve port on the truck jammed right into my radiator. As the gas man chuckled, he said, "Young man, that is not the gas tank." I got my gas then drove back up the hill with a badly leaking radiator. Now I had another problem—Pa was expecting me to pick him up when he got off work, and my cell phone (ha) had "no service."

Like I said, I'm pretty inventive. I pulled the radiator off the Model-T and took it into town on my bike. The hole was large enough so I could slip it over the handlebar. I went to the shop and asked the mechanic if he could recore my radiator. He looked at the radiator hanging from my handlebar and rudely started laughing uncontrollably. He said, "I'm sorry, but I just never saw a leak quite this bad. And by the way, it can't be recored…you need a new one." This was not the news I was expecting, but I got my new hunk of brass and put Ole Betsey back together. Pa was not too happy, but when we got home and he had his supper and I told him the story, he lit a cigarette, poured a little brandy, and was in a better mood. I don't know if it was the "medication" or Ma's food, but he did seem to mellow a little.

Thrown a Rod Lately?

Good Ole Betsey kept me pretty busy. I remember one time a connecting rod came loose and gave new meaning to the mechanic's phrase "throwing a rod." The rod blew right through the oil pan, and when it hit the pavement, it hit with such force it looked like a bent kitchen spoon. I took a hammer, straightened it out, and reattached it. Now what do I do for the hole in the oil pan? I went to the house and got a canning lid, wrapped a rag around it, and screwed it into place. That lasted a while until I could afford a new oil pan.

Baking with Pa

One of Pa's night jobs was at a large bakery. Yah, Pa could bake. He would work in the mixing area, and I worked at the end of the oven. The ovens were long, and working there was best at night when the heat was less sweltering.

Working at a bakery had its benefits. The conveyor going through the oven became our coffee-break canteen. When it was time our buddies on the feed end would throw on a row of empty bread pans to signal that the coffee pot was right behind. We would "accidentally" damage a loaf or two of fresh, hot bread, smear it with butter, and with the freshly perked coffee, we were in heaven. Dunkin' Donuts couldn't light a candle compared to our canteen break.

Also, since Pa was well respected and his boss knew he had a big family, he would bring home a three-by-three-foot box of goodies once a week. It had just about any kind of baked goods you could think of. Pies, cakes, bread, cookies, you name it. Sweet treats galore! Of course, these were yesterday's surplus, but who cares?

Cobbling—Putting One Foot in Front of the Other

Pa had many vocations. Growing up in Romania, he had learned the art of cobbling, making shoes from scratch. He'd make a pattern from the client's feet using newspaper then, using a wooden mold, would form the leather by moistening, stretching, and clamping it until it dried. A cobbler's hands are strong and rough. With simple hand tools, the leather becomes an art form. Later in life, Pa and I became a father-and-son shoemaking duo. In time we got machinery and found we could provide a necessary and respected service to the community. I was so intrigued by the process and found such joy in repairing, restyling, and in some cases repurposing leather products. When I felt I was ready to take the next step, I set up a shoe shop of my own in my garage to help provide extra income for my growing family.

Years later I had a two-car, cement-block garage built on the corner lot next to our house and finally had an operation I was proud of. I called my shop Shoe Repairing by Raleigh, and my motto for advertising was "A man is known by the footprints he leaves." Special community needs allowed me to use the innovative skills God gave me. I would make belly pads for men that buffed chrome trim for the Big Three. These were made from old leather machinery belting and Army surplus web belts. I would have to strip the dirt and oil from the belting before starting since it carried evidence of a past life. Heavy canvas became rivet pouches for iron workers. I also fabricated safety harnesses for dirt track race drivers. My inventions, although crude and basic, did provide safety for the drivers at the speed they traveled back then. You may even see some of my creations in the Henry Ford (or NASCAR) museums… Maybe not. My engineering skills were tested with prescriptions for orthopedic shoe modifications. I could rarely read the doctor's scriptwriting, but I was able to follow their sketches and measurements. In my spare time, I would made those round, leather fold-up change purses and custom-embossed leather belts. Leather was my life, and I was proud of every creation, whether it be a special item or just a pair of new soles on a businessman's dress shoes. "Prime" material was the only kind of leather I would use. Some shoemakers would try to keep the cost down by purchasing the less expensive grades, but like Pa, I believed that the beauty and endurance of quality materials was appreciated. I would have a constant stream of work from every corner of the community from the local cops to the mayor. Mayor Bates's son was in the Secret Service in Washington, DC, and when he came home, he would drop in to get his footwear reheeled and soled. The "prime" stamp on the leather soles was a badge of honor, and every cobbler leaves his trademark in the pride of his workmanship. Like an artist, there is a certain way you personally do the work, but then there is also the number of nails you use and the pattern they are set in on the sole. I suppose a cobbler could be traced by a good detective; the technique would be like dental records in establishing the workman that last fixed the shoes. Who knows, you may also get some of his DNA from minor cuts from the sharp knives they use.

Thinking of the mayor's son, I often wondered where those shoes led him. Did he walk the halls of the White House? Did they take him into the inner sanctum of the West Wing? Was he assigned to work the Treasury and actually see up close millions of uncut one-hundred-dollar bills? Or did he oversee the burning of the torn and tattered currency as it ended its long journey? I never knew because I was respectful of his position, and then again…he was Secret Service, and he would probably have to shoot me if he answered my questions.

The Book's Title

As for the title of this book—by now you may wonder what this book title is all about. If you know anything about cobblers, you'd know that they work with a lot of tiny nails. I keep them handy by putting them in my mouth, and with my tongue, I'd position the mini spikes and maintain supply in a rhythm that would make Ringo Star jealous. If I felt a sneeze coming on, I'd quickly empty the reservoir. In my case, I'm right-handed, so I would move the tacks from my mouth with my left hand. My right hand was the worker, but it's buddy (Mr. Left) took all the abuse. The cobbler's hammer has a wide head with a "nonskid" base. I have big hands with large fingers, and my left thumb was always getting whacked…*ouch*. Anybody got a Band-Aid? It seems I always had a damaged thumbnail, and one was either in the process of coming or going.

Another trademark is a shoemaker's hands and arms. They are strong! Cutting thick leather and rubber builds the hands. In my prime my friends knew my handshake might end up inflicting pain, but new acquaintances were handled more gingerly.

Over the years, as God graced us with a growing family, I had to take on more and more "side jobs" to make ends meet. Seemingly, whenever I thought I could make ends meet… someone moved the ends.

Other than the US Rubber and Bethesda Missionary Temple main jobs, I took on many small private jobs such as tiling basements, plumbing, electrical, tearing down buildings, selling Filter Queen Vacuum Cleaners, cleaning a bank branch, and cleaning mobile home models and installing commercial drapery for school stages.

The Bank Caper

I remember a couple of incidents while working at the bank. I worked in the evening, after closing hours, dusting, cleaning restrooms, mopping, and waxing throughout. One night I found a very large money sack next to the teller area. Everyone had left, and I notified the branch manager by phone. That sack should have been secured in the safe at end of day, and needless to say, he appreciated my honesty. It could have cost him his job if the bag had been "lost." But then there was another time when he didn't really appreciate the extra effort I took. You see, I noticed his desk chair's wheels were squeaking and would barely roll. I took the time to clean the wheels and oil them. Mr. Foch had the habit of landing on the chair a little hard, and with the free-wheeling, he almost ended up in the parking lot. He enjoyed the new feel of the chair, but he asked me to leave him a warning note if I did things that might alter his slant on life.

Picking
The Cash Stash

And then there was "picking." This was way before there was any such thing known as a picker. Nowadays some may have labeled me as a hoarder… Not so. I just grew up in a time when people knew how to make things work. Trouble is, my working stock kept growing, and time to complete projects was minimal… There was an old man (yeah, much older than me). He lived across from the church where I worked and was Polish (as if that makes a difference.) He asked me to cut down a large apple tree in his backyard. So I bought a brand-new Homelite sixteen-inch chainsaw, and my son Jimmy and I got started taking down this big apple tree. It had taken on some disease, and the old man was afraid it would come down by itself, and anyway, I could use the wood for our fireplace. All was going well. We buzzed off the main limbs and started on the trunk. Then sparks started to fly, literally. The old man forgot to tell me that his wife had been dropping stones into the hollow of the tree to keep the squirrels out. Well, the job took much longer than expected with all the resharpening of the chain we had to do. As I cut the grass at the church, I would also cut his. He had a postage-stamp-sized lot, so the favor was quick and easy, and he and his wife appreciated the gesture. Well, over time his wife became ill and passed away. Later the old man was in the hospital. I visited him and continued to cut his grass so he could come home to a maintained yard. You see, he had no one. His daughter lived out of state. The old man's condition seemed to worsen, and he never came home. One day after passing away, his attorney came by to see me. It seems that the man had given orders that I be given everything he had as a thank-you for years of friendship and service, and his only daughter lived out of state and wanted nothing. I was surprised, to say the least. So one day Jimmy and I went over with a trailer and did some picking. The garage was full of yard tools, and there were tools in the basement also. As we looked around, we found rags stuffed into the basement floor joists and under a canning crock. These rags were protecting some US saving bonds dating back to the midforties. The total face value was about $3,000, but adding interest would bring the value much higher. We were on the hunt. Jimmy found a bathtub faucet repair access in a closet and removed the door. Inside were two-quart jars filled with silver coins. I took all the bonds and coins over to his lawyer, and the counselor said they were legally mine. In my heart I felt that the daughter should receive these items, and I instructed the lawyer to make sure she had them to remember her parents.

Mixed Signals

I told a friend that I was looking for a woodburning kitchen cook stove for the cottage. He said, "If you'd like to take a drive out into the country, I know a farmer that has one for sale, and he wants $15 for it." It sounded like a good deal, so I called the farmer and hooked up my trailer for my pig-in-a-poke purchase. You can't buy an antique stove like that for $200, much less $15. We arrived at the farm, and the farmer directed us to a shed in the middle of the field. I thought, "This can't be good." Oh, ye of little faith! The shed door swung open as the rusty hinges creaked, and there it stood in all its glory. It was a Detroit brand combination wood/gas kitchen cook stove with a backsplash, warming shelf, and water-heating reservoir. Boy, what a find. There was no question—this stove was perfect for what we needed, and I said to the farmer, "I understand you are asking $15 for the stove." He responded, "That's right, if you wait right here, I'll go get it." Wow, not only was the price awesome, but he was going to pay me to haul it off. I told him, "No, no, I'm going to pay you $15 for it." He looked a bit puzzled, but then smiled as I peeled off three fives.

Weathered Leather

When a good friend Mike Branzak passed away, his widow Gertrude called and asked me to come over to his garage and take whatever I could use. She was trying to downsize, and one of her chores was to discard what her husband had acquired over the years. Mike was also in the leather business, such as me. He had worked for Packard Motorcar in the upholstery line and had many tools and leather scraps from the high-quality seating and trim that adorned these classic vehicles. Many of the tools Mike had, he made himself. There were handmade knives and chisels formed from ground down files and fitted with handles of wood or aluminum. I found general tools of the trade that I was well acquainted with. A hand-cranked skive for beveling leather and many knives, trimmers, and all sorts of leather finishing tools. Mike also had collected a stash of prime leather strips in the Packard trim colors.

This "pick" was one of my most treasured and provided memories of a great friend and our times together.

Slightly Soiled

Then there was the time my brother Wally came across some furniture being discarded by the Downtown Detroit YMCA. This furniture was so well built it could support an elephant. The armchairs were extremely heavy, and the vinyl fabric seemed indestructible, but it was badly soiled. Back in those days, smoking was allowed, and the chairs had an off-white look as to color—way…off-white! We tried cleaners and scrubbing till our shoulders hurt. Then I used a toxic stripper I used in my shop for taking glue off shoes. I got it down to the bare white, but the fumes got me to seeing pink elephants, and they were getting oozy too. All in all, the chairs added sturdy seating in our family room for many years.

Treasure to Firewood

Another friend, who will remain nameless, not because I can't remember his name but because it brings back bad memories of a pick that went south. You see, George had this antique sofa bed he wanted to get rid of. It was in his basement. This had to be a first-generation sofa bed… And I do mean first-generation! Its frame was very heavy oak with arms that were massive and wide. The foldout bed was heavy iron, and the mattress support was heavy grade springs and wire. All in all, it took three men and a boy to get it out of the basement, and when it came to putting it into our family room, I almost lost it. It was so big and massive we had to totally dismantle it to get it through the doors. The cushions were heavy gauge leather and filled with horsehair and might also have been originally used at the Y—where I got its babies. This was a bad pick. We never got a decent mattress, and since no one would even sit on it because it was so uncomfortable, it became firewood.

A Missionary Couple's Dilemma

Our church was founded with the Ministry of World Missions. Over the years, pastors were sent all over the world to share the Good News as the Lord called them. There were missions in Africa, Europe, Central America, and other mission fields. There was a couple in their senior years that were heading to Israel. The Wilsons were a special couple, and their departure date was rapidly approaching. They were packed with all that they would be taking, but they had a problem. They were turning their house over to the new owners on Monday, and they had a *few things* yet to dispose of. They called me and asked if I could come over and help dispose of their surplus. And it was surplus. You see, "Scoop" had worked for the railroad, and he loved the salvage auctions they held to dispose of damaged and unclaimed items. Now the volume Scoop had was unreal, and he had to get rid of it all in two days. Long story short, there was a drill press, antique canoe sailing rig, antique hand-made riding boots, and hundreds of other things. We loaded a bunch, then noticed heavy wooden boxes. They contained tons of grinding wheels. Jimmy's eyes lit up. You see, he saw the possibility of marketing them to businesses and maybe financing his college education. We hauled several loads from the west side of Detroit to Warren, and when we were finally done, my yard looked like "Scoop's" before we picked it. The grinding wheels were all different diameters, different grits, and different arbor sizes. Some of them were three feet in diameter with two-foot arbor openings. Jim contacted dozens of companies and eventually found that because of new OSHA requirements, none of the tons of wheels we had could be used. They were old and lacked the identifying markings as to grit, type of use, or max safe RPM speed. Do I have to take them to the dump and pay a dumping fee? Nope! I just widened my driveway by inserting the smaller wheels inside the larger ones and covering them with gravel. Problem solved, and profit lost!

Repurposing

Repurposing became my way of life. I would use discarded aluminum storm windows for the cottage. I mounted them inside and out. They weren't pretty, and they sure weren't insulated, but this was for a summer cottage, and they were free! Discarded bricks, after old mortar was removed, became chimneys and a fireplace. A wide concrete step became a fireplace mantle. Wood of every type, size, and length was denailed and stacked. Even used drywall took its place on walls. The irregular shapes and angles weren't a problem; you just have to be creative in your reinstallation. Remember, an inexpensive paneling or wallpaper can cover most any base surface, and I did my best to keep Michigan "green"! Remember all those nails that got pulled from the used lumber? I had my sons use an anvil and hammer to straighten them out for further use. I didn't tell them that a bent and restraightened nail isn't worth a flip. They'll bend as you try to use them, especially in the petrified old boards, but it did keep them busy and out of my hair for a few hours.

Brute Strength

Then there was the family project that I and my sons took on at the church. They had an old, large coal boiler that needed to be removed from its basement location to make room for a new modern one. This was a big project! The boiler was about eight feet wide, ten feet tall, and about sixteen feet long and was totally cast iron. By us doing the work, the church would save a lot of money on the project, and we could scrap the iron. It was an enormous job. We used sledgehammers and carried each and every piece up to a large truck parked in the alley. At the end of the day and two loads to the scarp yard later, we were very tired, but the job was done. I took the whole family to Singing Sam's Italian Restaurant for supper one night. We had a good meal, Dena didn't have to cook, Singing Sam did what he did best, and as a family we enjoyed an unusual night on the town… And we had a little extra that week for our budget.

Progress? Not So Much

This new generation needs a calculator, PC, iPod, Nook, notebook, and state-of-the-art 4G LTE cell phone. It just boggles my mind. And when these fail, they throw them out and go buy another. Back in my day, you could fix things. I believe that if man-made it, I could fix it. Things aren't made to fix anymore. Everything is a throwaway. Have you looked under the hood of your car lately? Try fixing it yourself. You'll need more than a canning lid and a rag to plug a leaking oil pan, I guarantee it! My backyard mechanic used to time my engine, not even with a timing light, but by watching the radio antenna. He would rotate the distributor cap until the antenna stopped vibrating. Now there is no antenna, no points or timing to adjust, and all you can do is watch for the idiot light that tells you to "whip out your wallet." Even the simple things like changing your own oil are harder to do yourself than it should be. Special tools are needed to remove the old filter. But even in yesteryear, if I had a problem removing my old filter with a wrench, I could take a screwdriver and whack it with a hammer and provide an alternative way to get the stubborn filter loose. Now they hide the filter up into the maze of hoses, pipes, and whatever so that unless you have that *special* wrench…you're out of luck. Then what about the myriad of hand tools. It used to be that a flat blade, Phillip's head, crescent wrench, and a set of ASE sockets would suffice to do fix almost anything. Now there are metrics, square drive, hex drive, star drive, Allen drive. I can only think of one reason to muddy the tool waters, and that's so you never have the right tool to address even the easiest repairs…

Give me a Model-T and a supply of canning lids and rags any day.

The Custodian of God's House

For over thirty-two years, I was privileged to be custodian and head of general maintenance for one of the fastest-growing and eventually one of the largest houses of worship in the country. Though all the building, acquisition, demolition, and rebuilding projects kept my interest, the need to keep an active church clean and organized, while keeping my religion, I can only give credit to my God and my dear wife Dena.

Can you imagine the immenseness of such responsibility? Every day I did all I could within my God-given ability and strength. So many stories could be written about that thirty-two years, but I will select a few to highlight my tenure as a man with a mission.

I sincerely believe that God placed me there, and little did I know that this was to be more than just a job with a paycheck.

Mopping, stripping, waxing, buffing, and vacuuming floors was continual. Setting up for the various services and tending to the doors and windows at the entrances was routine.

Bethesda had seasonal conventions each year, and it seemed that from time to time, something would be the high mark of each revival. Besides the infamous Spirit-filled services, much happened behind the scenes. I would often see attendees pass me as they would go inside with some carrying humongous leather briefcases. Maybe they were carrying a change of clothes, lunch, or whatever. I wished they would come with empty ones and take back with them the knowledge God gave them to take home.

Hey, Buddy, Can You Spare Me a Dime?

There was this one well-dressed guy. He was very professional-looking. He was seen sharing his "misfortune" with others and was able to con many into helping him financially. You should have seen the expression on the face of the intended mark when he attempted to deny the help by indicating that all he had was a twenty-dollar bill. Then the beggar whipped out a wad of money to make change. This guy did not have a hotel room but was sleeping in a boxcar down by Davison and Van Dyke. Everybody, and even I, felt sorry for him at first. One morning he asked me if I would allow him to make his breakfast on my hot plate in the janitor's room. Well, I went my way to do things and later passed by the room and saw Mr. Daily cooking kidneys (without first cleaning them) and after dicing them added oatmeal. The smell was putrid! A little while later, the pastor's husband came downstairs and said to me, "What is that—that smell?" You see, at that time, Pop wasn't walking the walk yet but got his point across. I told him what I allowed this guy to do, and Pop took care of the problem in short order.

Music to My Ears

Then there was the time I got in early, and as I entered the building, I heard music. I presumed that one of the secretaries had left the radio on in the second-floor office. As I got up to the second level, I noticed the music coming from higher up. I got to the third level, which was the top of the balcony, and yet the music was still coming from higher up. There was a prayer tower at the next level up. That was the only thing up there, and it also allowed access to the roof through a window. This convention night service "leftover" had hidden in the immense building, and after everyone had left, he had free reign of God's house. He took his trumpet to the roof and decided to serenade the community with his music. I'm sure those at street level thought the heavenly music was a gift from God Almighty… But really, it was a man without enough money to get a room for the night.

The Bad Samaritan

Then there was the time I was shoveling a deep snowfall, trying to prepare the entrances for a morning service. The weather was cold, but I was working up a sweat. Then up came a man dressed to the nines and said, "Brother Rollo, I'm going to go in and pray for you." I told him, "I appreciate your prayers, but I have another shovel against the wall." He turned and continued his search for the Lord's way.

On His Knees

Whenever you have a prosperous church, there are those wanting to take whatever they can, and our church was no exception. One morning I found the office door broken, as was the inner storeroom door. I found the large safe severely damaged, but not opened. A call to the police, and their review revealed this large safe was just minutes away from being opened. They searched the area and found the thief crouched between the seats in the auditorium with the evidential hammer in his hand. In his kneeling position, maybe he was praying he wouldn't be caught or maybe asking God for mercy.

My family knew that the cobbler spends time on his knees, sometimes between the rows of the sanctuary, talking to his true friend and finding direction for his chores, and more importantly, for handling the day-to-day problems of raising a large family.

Thief Comes Out of the Closet

Years later security problems continued, and we hired a night watchman. The pastors thought of arming him, but considering his poor eyesight, it might be counterproductive. They opted to provide him a "guard dog." The watchman and the dog went through training, and finally the security team was complete. Then one Sunday night, the soundman and the watchman were in the pastor's office (which doubled as a sound control room for the church and radio station). The church was locked up, with lights turned off, and they were just killing a little time. I guess they were there about a half hour when Sheba walked in from the dark auditorium. She would lie in the rear of the middle aisle just doing what she was supposed to do. Well, she walked into the office, went straight to the closet, stood, and growled at the door. Carefully the watchman opened the door to find a thief with knife in hand looking at a large German Shepherd with her teeth showing and a growl that meant business. The Men in Blue came and rescued the guy from his tormentor.

The Lock Swap

Then was the time when somehow a lock master key got out and we had to change all the lock cylinders. What a massive and fast-paced operation had to take place. I coordinated with the locksmith and would take ten locks at a time and pick up the ten he fixed, then take ten more until we were done. Security is always an issue.

The Basement Church, No More

I guess the most serious incident was when the Basement Church (as we called it) caught fire and threatened the main auditorium. The fire totaled the basement, and the smoke and water was very damaging to the rest of the church. That project was long and hard to restore the church for use. The cause of the fire was determined to be a lightning strike on a rooftop air-conditioning duct. But there is more to this story. That night there was a visiting preacher that prophesied that lightning would strike the building. After that fire I don't remember him ever being invited to preach there again, but that might just be a coincidence.

Picnic Anyone?

One of our annual events was the July 4 Sunday school picnic. At first, they were at a farm. There we had to bring tables, chairs, and set up outhouses. We would also hang large US Army canvas water dispensers which would be filled with a block of ice and water and had four spigots for dispensing. Mr. Peters was a Twin Pines milkman and provided milk and ice cream cups for the kids. In later years arrangements were made with the Lutheran Institute for the Deaf, which was just a couple blocks west of our church and had acreage on their campus for our picnics. There we didn't have to set up outhouses, and they had electricity available. Such progress!

The High-Flying Piano

During one of the many expansion projects, the church built a second-story addition to the gymnasium. It was attached to the original storefront building in which the church had its beginnings. It was a beautiful "Upper Room" and was the home of the catechism class. The annual student count was over one hundred kids per year, and over the years the curriculum has changed the lives of tens of thousands. Understanding God was seen to be an effective primer to eleven- to thirteen-year-olds and then was expanded to also have adult classes. My wife, Dena, was a coteacher with the program founder Patricia Beall-Gruits for about thirty years.

Well, a piano was donated for the room, but there was no way to get it upstairs. The indoor stairway had landings too small to allow turning the oversize instrument, but with any problem there is a solution, some not as safe as others.

The church treasurer had a business a couple of miles away and said he could bring a forklift and a bunch of pallets. He would lift the piano on some pallets, then put more underneath, and keep going until the necessary height was reached.

Oh boy! The height was much higher than a normal second story, and as the Leaning Tower of Piano grew and grew, it looked like the machine operator might have a headache…and he didn't even have a hard hat on. Finally, the piano was at the proper height and needed to be taken off the lift and scooted into the room. The "engineers" downstairs had me wrap a rope around the heavy floating music box and tie it to myself to secure it. The tug-of-war was on, and I'm glad God was my anchorman.

The Custodian's "Office"

My office was the janitor's room in the basement. I had built a wall cabinet, which had a small foldout table on which I set my lunch and coffee-break goodies. The cabinet had shelves inside to stock a small supply of simple, single-serving foods.

My workbench sported a vise and a hot plate. There were tools, paints, cleaners for whatever maintenance was needed. I found an old scissor-type mirror which could be extended to see myself as others would see me. Over time I added a discarded recliner. A Bible was stashed on the bottom shelf of my cabinet, and I would read during my break or during lunch. I usually had time for a short nap before returning to my fast-paced chores. I also had a clean shirt and tie hanging behind my office door. You see, I wasn't just a janitor, but also an elder. There were times when a person would come by the church hoping to catch a minister, and at least one was on-site most of the time. But then there were times when I would get a call from the office secretary asking me to fill in and assist someone with an urgent need, and no pastor in house.

I remember this one occasion when a distraught man needed someone to talk with. He was on his way to commit suicide and saw the church. I quickly changed my shirt and brought him down to my office. We talked for quite some time as I shared the Word from my Bible and personal experiences. We prayed, and the man left my office changed in mind and spirit. This man became a long-term member of the church and God's family. That day was the first day of the rest of his life, but it was just another day in the life of a church custodian. I treasured my opportunity to minister not only one-on-one, but also to the whole church as I prepared it for God's next infilling.

Things have changed, the church has relocated to Sterling Heights, but the memories of the beginning years are cherished by all.

Dena, the Cook's Cook

I know many very small families who did not customarily eat their daily meals around the dinner table. There may be such a simple reason—maybe the meals presented were not well-thought-out, or maybe the cook may have never developed skills necessary to place scrumptious, tasty food before the family.

Having a large family and limited income to provide good nutritious food, cooking is a skill that Dena learned at an early age.

I remember her having me subscribe to the *Sunday Detroit News*, which was loaded with advertisements and coupons. Dena would go through page by page, selecting those items that would fill her basket with the basics of the week's meals. Our shopping day was spent going store to store in search of the needed components.

Since Dena didn't drive, at first I was the one to take her on her weekly trek. Then one by one the kids would take Mom to search for the items she needed. It seems that the last kid to get their license didn't seem to mind driving. We could always say they were honing much-needed skills, while giving me time to work on shoes out in my shop. When I drove her, I would sit out in the car, awaiting her return with a basket full. I would start out reading the paper (around the holes from the missing coupons), then would use that paper to cover my eyes while I took a little catnap. Soon a tap on the window would set me in motion loading the car. Dena seemed okay with me staying outside, since when I accompanied her, we seemed to spend more. But then, when the kids drove and went in with her, they might pick a thing or two which wasn't on the list, and she just adjusted the list a little.

Dena could make something out of nothing, make enough to feed the gang, and yet have a little leftover for a quick lunch.

Although Pa and I had baking experience, I tried to keep out of her way in the kitchen. My annual joy was making a cornucopia for the family Thanksgiving table. I made it out of a superlong strip of bread dough shaped around a crinkled tin foil mold, then baked to perfection. On the table we would fill it with fresh fruit to overflowing, showing God's bounty and blessing.

Dena began sharing her kitchen skills early in our kids' elementary school when they were looking for a kitchen chairman. She would oversee kitchen operation for school parties and events.

That experience led her in later years to cater for our church dinners, parties, and wedding receptions. I remember a wedding that was held on the West Side of Detroit. The couple wanted canopies (miniature sandwiches) as an appetizer. Dena made homemade bread, but since presentation was important to her, she added food coloring to the dough and alternated colors top and bottom, which made beautiful mini sandwiches. That meal was so beautiful but so much work that she didn't do it again.

Dena and I made a good catering team, and having a large family, we never seemed to lack in finding the labor to help in the kitchen, serve, clean up, and do the dishes. Back then we seldom used paper plates, nor did we have commercial dish-washers—all work was done by "Arm-Strong."

Most all our family meals were capped by some type of desert. Jell-O, cake, pie, cookies—anything to show that little extra effort in making us all happy.

Dena was known for her strudel. She would make the dough and put it in a very large cast aluminum Silver Seal pot with a lid. She then put it in the kids' bedroom on their bed, covered by blankets, to aid the yeast in rising. After punching it down a time or two, she would parse it and begin her stretch-o-rama. Dena used a clean bedsheet to cover the table. Starting with a round dough disk about ten inches in diameter, she would walk round and round the table, gently pulling and stretching until it was paper thin and the edges lapped over the table's edge. Then she removed the tough edge all the way around and set it aside. Later she would roll the ends, cut them in four-inch disks, and fry them as elephant ears, a treat for the kids.

The next step was to drizzle melted butter across the stretched dough, spread the filling with cheese, nuts/sugar/raisins, sweet cabbage, which we called "krout," apple, cherry, or any other filling she might have. Then Dee would flip in the sides and begin rolling the filled dough by grabbing the sheet and flip, flip, and flip until the roll was complete. The four-foot-long roll was then snaked onto a cookie sheet for baking.

Faith and Myrtle would have "strudel parties." Several girls would come over for tutoring by Dena and would then invite their boyfriends over when finished to sample what they had made.

Since making strudel was so time-consuming, she always made the effort worthwhile by making several different kinds at one time. There was always enough to send some home with dinner guests.

Another one of her specialties was her "Christmas cake." This is actually a cookie-type dough on the top and bottom with sugar and chopped nuts as the filling. A topping of egg whites and sugar made this a scrumptious dessert but was reserved for Christmastime.

My specialty was preparing the pot roast for Sunday dinner. Dena was getting all the kids ready for church, so I made our lunch. We had an electric stove, so leaving it on while we went to church was no problem; all I had to do was set the timer.

My other specialty was my barbecues. I was the "grill master" before anyone ever used that title. Dena made her home sauce from a secret recipe, and the ribs were made with love and skill.

When out-of-town preachers came together for our church revivals, we would have our pastors and the visitors over for dinner. I remember one time it started to pour down rain while I was grilling. That particular grill was in the shape of a wishing well and had a removable rooftop, so we put the top back on, and we put the boat tarp across the clotheslines so I could stay near my cooking. It turned out to be a very good dinner.

Like they say, "The way to a man's heart is through his stomach," and I believe there is something to that.

The Cobbler's Crooner Years

I can't say too much about dating, having little or no money, and I guess I was somewhat afraid. I was always working and, when not working, was spending my time pursuing my dream of being a good musician. I loved guitars and acquired many. I had mandolins, banjos, acoustic, German steel guitar, which was embossed with lilies of the valley. I also played a wicked harmonica.

I developed a love of the music of the islands. There was just something so soothing with its special tone and the ability to play a guitar on your lap. In my mind's eye, I could only dream of being among the orchids, flowers, and birds singing harmony to tunes as I stroked on my Varga Hawaiian guitar.

In Pa's shoe shop, I would build models of ships I saw in magazines and sold them to fund my purchase of guitars and music. Ofttimes I would take my younger sister Julia to Belle

Isle and rent a canoe. We'd float around the lagoon as I sang and rehearsed my acoustic guitar pickings.

Here was this tall, lanky guy with a slightly younger girl floating around in their own little world, oblivious to those around them, but providing a musical interlude for their enjoyment. Little did they know the girl was my sister.

Ma and Pa made sure us kids all got to church on Sundays (as well as other days). I found a church is a good place which provides an audience when you are learning music. Unlike other places where things may be thrown at you when you miss a note, or pluck the wrong string, church people are usually forgiving.

As a young man entering that awkward time of choosing a prospect to be my lifelong mate, I prayed long and hard. You see, I didn't want to face a future of living with someone who was not God's choice for me, and you can only know who that is when you put it in His hands.

I told my Heavenly Father, "I don't want my eyes to deceive me, I don't want to make the choice for my future, I want You to make it. I will know it is Your choice when the girl asks me to marry her when I have nothing to offer."

To many this might seem stupid. Does God have a sense of humor, and would He set me up with a plain Jane, or would He give me His best?

Well, this one Sunday I was in the front row of a small church with my laptop Hawaiian guitar (hooked up to a portable amplifier) and accompanied the pianist with traditional

Sunday morning music. I noticed that there was a visiting evangelistic minister that Sunday. She was very pretty, and I tried so hard not to look up anytime during the service. I was trusting God, but it was not easy to avoid eye contact.

After the service, I busied myself putting my instrument in its case and hauling it out to the car. Yep, I was avoiding any contact.

We headed home, and Ma was making our Sunday dinner when there was a knock at the front door. I answered it to find on the other side was the beauty I was trying to squash from my mind. Here, Ma had invited this visiting evangelist to have lunch with our family. With eleven in the family already, Ma was trying to set me up with the "right woman." Was it to reduce her food bills, or was God whispering in her ear, "Here she is"?

Well, long story short, we dated for a little while, mostly to church services and social functions. Everywhere we went, we took the streetcar. Everyone seems to think that electric energy is something new, but back then streetcars had railroad tracks down the middle of most major streets in Detroit, and then later, electric-powered buses were commonplace with their roof-mounted booms connected to overhead power sources.

We palled around and went ice and roller-skating and got to know the most direct streetcar routes to wherever we went. I would pick her up, go to church, then take her home, and missing a connection every now and then, I sometimes got Dena home a little later then her mother thought reasonable. It got to a point that one day her Ma said to her, "Marry him or break it off." Wow!

So here, when I had nothing to offer the most beautiful girl in the world, she asked me, "Raleigh, will you marry me?"

It was the question I was waiting to hear from someone, and hearing it coming from her gave me the confidence in God's wisdom and provision for any decision I was to make in the future.

PS. By the way, I said, *yes!*

Words from the Cobbler's Wife

They say that behind every good man stands a woman. Then I guess, beside every good cobbler stands his wife holding his right hand. Raleigh and I have been holding hands for over sixty-six years. Through the years we experienced joy, sorrow, poverty, and blessing, but we wouldn't have changed one moment.

Some would say that's ridiculous, but when you truly love each other, you can endure all things with God's unfailing grace and mercy.

Our wedding day was very memorable. Raleigh and I are descendants of immigrants, and as such, our families were poor, although at that time, everyone we knew were in somewhat the same boat (literally).

My mother, Rucia (Mary), and Dad, Paul, came over from Hungary. She was born in Iska and migrated to America. I was born in Detroit, Michigan. Ma never went to school and couldn't read nor write, so helping them in their daily lives fell on me, being the eldest of the five children. I had two brothers, Johnny and Paul, and two sisters, Florence and Virginia. Ma was a seamstress and also a good housekeeper. Pa worked for Henry Ford earning $5 a day in the factory and also a janitor at Park Davis, a well-known Detroit pharmaceutical manufacturer.

With Ma's homemaking skills, and the need to add income to the family coffer, she took in up to twenty boarders at a time. Ten worked the early shift, and the other ten the night shift, so they shared sleeping arrangements. They all worked at the same factory as Pa, so they slept, ate, traveled, and worked as a well-oiled (fed) and tuned factory group.

You can only imagine the work she took on. Ma would wash clothes for them all on a scrubboard, boiling the extra dirty ones on a boiler. The meals looked like she was feeding an army.

Later we moved to a smaller place, large enough for just our family. Ma dug up part of the backyard and planted dill (bosivc), parsley, tomatoes, basil, and peppers. When our plants were big enough, I would carry them around in a little red wagon Ma had bought me. She got me a wooden grape box we loaded up with our baby plants we raised from seed.

Ma had a secret ingredient to spurn growth to the seedlings we were to later sell. You see, back then grocery stores basically came to your front door. Vendors had horse-drawn carts carrying many fresh fruits, vegetables, ice, milk and dairy, and fish products, etc. There were also Sheenies who would pick up all types of scrap metal, appliances, and newspapers. Sheeny is a slang and contemptuous name given poor Jewish entrepreneurs in days past. These vendors usually had a bugle or trumpet to alert the neighborhood they were there to service their needs. Most times those horses left behind litter in the way of dung, which was one of their drawbacks. Ma would go out every morning with her special broom and shovel to collect the nutrients needed for our seedling garden. There is always a downside…the horse manure is loaded with undigested weed seed, and we always had extra weeding to do. Ma's personal fruits veggies were the biggest and best in the neighborhood.

I would walk to Eastern Market on Gratiot where farmers rented stalls to sell their produce and freshly butchered meat. I would park my wagon at the end of the line of truck farmers and sell our plants for $.25 per bunch of twelve plant starters.

With the money, Ma would buy material and thread to sew dresses for us girls and shirts for Johnny and Paul. She would take us downtown and let us pick out the material, which made us feel so special.

Mom never went to school, and her inability to read or write kept her from using sewing patterns, so she would go to stores or magazines and go home and cut her own patterns out of newspaper. If we already had a dress we liked, she would take it apart and size it a little bigger to fit. Ma had an old treadle sewing machine which she could run as if it had a motor.

Paul and Florence never married. They made a great uncle and aunt for our family's children. Virginia married and had one son. Johnny, who died young of a heart attack, married Margaret Dikin (Raleigh's sister), and they had nine children. Johnny's family, being the largest in the Dikin clan, put a heavy load on Macci when John passed away. There was so much to do, education-wise, social-wise, and overall just raising nine kids. Sometimes they had a couple in diapers or potty training at one time. Like I mentioned, Uncle Paul and Aunt Flo were very much a part of that household.

For entertainment, my mother would take small pebbles and teach us how to play jacks with them. Later we ended up buying a real set of jacks, but we also enjoyed skipping rope. Ma would take an end of a rope (which doubled as a clothes-line), and my sister would turn the other end. We got to where we could jump different steps and run through without touch-ing the rope. Then we raised the rope higher and higher to see just how high we could jump without touching the rope. At the same time, my brothers had fun with their friends playing marbles.

Ma always wanted us girls to have something special, and she taught us how to crochet frilly tops for our slips. We also embroidered dresser scarfs, pillowcases, and tablecloths. We always had something to do, and she enjoyed seeing what we could accomplish. Looking back, we enjoyed so many things during a poverty-stricken time in our lives.

It just proves that you don't always need expensive toys to have fun. You seldom hear of this type to enjoyment these days.

Growing Up with My Brother Johnny

I remember growing up with my brother John Butzu. I remember when we lived downriver, on Maple Street. At that time, we went to Brownson Grade School and attended the Greek Orthodox church. We attended the Romanian church, but mostly just on holidays. I remember that church had so many icons, statutes, and banners all over the sanctuary.

In the fall, they had a fall festival at a hall. They would have a heavy rope strung all around with all sorts of fruit suspended by heavy strings. The men would bring their children and lift them up on their shoulders and let the kids pick their own fruit. We would pay $0.25 for each fruit we cut off. There were apples, pears, grapes, etc., and the proceeds went to the church's association.

When we lived on Maple Street, Johnny had some boyfriends that were black. They played together after school. These boy's fathers made barbecue every Friday night on a tin barrel and grill rack. Oh, the smell as it wafted down the street. The neighborhood was filled with the aroma like none other. The kids' mothers would also bake fresh bread and for $0.25, you would get a section of ribs and a slice of homemade bread. Dad would buy two every Friday night, and we were in heaven.

One day we started going to the Third Romanian Baptist Church on Lafayette near Chene Street, and after a while Pa got a part-time janitor job there. Pa was a very sincere and devoted man and loved the Lord with a truly deep love. Every night following supper, he would take his Bible and read out loud.

Pa was not a well person but was suffering from rheumatism. His illness was severe, and he would miss work a lot. There was a time that he was sick in bed almost a full year, not being able to bathe, eat, or clothe himself without help. Ma struggled to keep the family together during that trying time.

Later, when Pa was feeling a little better and was able to again return to work, he saved $100 for a down payment on a brand-new home for us. They were building the Kowalski Homes on Fenlon Street, and the price was $5,999, with payments of $59 per month. He and Ma decided that was what the family needed, so they bought one.

We still went to the Third Romanian Baptist Church on Sundays, and after a large dinner, Pa would lie down to rest. Us kids would go outside to play and soon learned that there was a woman in our neighborhood who had Sunday school in her home every Sunday afternoon. One day we went to see what it was all about, and when we knocked on her door, we were

greeted by a sweet tall lady. She was dressed in a white uni-
form-type dress and wore black oxfords. Her hair was done up
in a bun, but she had such a kind, smiling face. She invited us
in. Her living room was set up with rows of folding chairs, and
in the dining room she had an old-fashioned organ. We sang
songs, and she taught Bible stories.

When we came home, Dad asked us where we had gone,
and we told him of our newfound friend. Dad did his homework and found that the lady in white was a Pentecostal, and
he forbade us to go anymore. Of course, we disobeyed him
and continued going and attending every Sunday while he was
asleep. Well, Pa found out and quit going to church altogether.
He said, "I cannot be a deacon (which he was) and have my
children disobey me." He stayed home for three months, then
one Sunday morning, he called all us kids together and told us
to get ready, we were going to church. We were so happy to see
Dad was again going to church, but while on the streetcar, I
noticed the clock. It was near eleven o'clock, and I said, "Dad,
when we get there, the service will be over." He was furious and
said, "Dena, you must have tinkered with the clock." To this
day, I do not know why the clock wasn't running right, but I
said, "Dad, you paid for the streetcar tickets, let's stay on and
go to the church in Highland Park." That was a Pentecostal
church, and he reluctantly listened to me. When we arrived, we
were greeted at the door by men that Pa actually knew. Brother
Cadariau (John and Joe's dad) extended hands of friendship,
and Pa was a little more comfortable. That particular Sunday

was Communion Sunday, and the minister, Brother Netza, said, "This is not our table, it's the Lord's table, and everyone is welcome to come and partake. If you have received the Lord as your Savior and were water-baptized, please join us." Dad went up to the alter and knelt down. As he did, a well of tears flowed from his eyes in what seemed to be a never-ending flow. He was trembling and began speaking in tongues; he had truly been baptized in the Holy Spirit. This seemed to be the first day of the rest of his life.

Johnny Gets Hurt

When Johnny was about four or five years old, we were playing hide-and-seek and having a lot of fun. The one that had to do the "seeking" would always be blindfolded, which seemed to keep the cheating under control.

On this particular day, it was Johnny's turn to be the blind-folded seeker.

It was also Ma's laundry day. When Ma washed clothes, she used a flat-topped woodburning stove to boil water in an oval copper boiler to remove badly soiled spots. She had just removed the boiler from the stove and set it on the floor so she could put more wood in the firebox. She went out to get the wood, and at that same time Johnny came into the kitchen and fell into the tub of scalding water, severely burning his hands. I believe his screams could be heard all the way to the Detroit River.

In those days we didn't go to the doctor much; instead Ma, being very quick to action and was skilled on how to treat burns with home remedies, covered the burns with homemade lard and kept them saturated in lard covered with gauze. Bandages had to be changed daily until the healing was complete. Johnny's pain seemed to last forever, and we all felt responsible for this senseless accident.

Today no one would think of such home health solutions, but back then the mother had to expect the unexpected and with coolness, compassion, and wisdom stand able to address emergencies as they occur. Mothers were the doctors of choice because back then there was no 911, or ambulances or trauma medical centers, and urgent care wasn't ever thought of. If it weren't for Ma's quick thinking, Johnny might have been wounded for life, or infection might have set in, and he might have lost the use of his hands forever.

Friends

If you make friends with your enemy,
Then you have no more enemies!

A Preacher and a Teacher

My years of Sunday school placed a desire to share God's love with others, and at age sixteen, I went away to Dayton, Ohio, to prepare for the ministry that I felt was upon my heart.

My schooling was cut short, and I had to return home when my dad's health turned bad. Even with my lack of completing seminary, I was invited to small churches to hold evangelistic meetings. Back then, female ministers were not very common, and many wondered if this young girl could light a candle when compared to men that preached the Word, but it wasn't me; it was the God in me.

At a storefront Pentecostal church where I preached, a young man played a Hawaiian steel guitar during the song service. After his performance, he sat in the congregation and would not look up at me.

After the meeting, a woman whom heard I was Romanian started a conversation. She was Hungarian and was married to a Romanian man, she said, and invited me to their home for the following week's Sunday dinner.

To my surprise, when I arrived at their house, the person who opened the door was the young musician who wouldn't look at me when I spoke at his church. He was the couple's oldest son, Raleigh (the cobbler, Aurel).

He started taking me to and from church on streetcars. Yes, those were our dates. Neither of us owned a car, because his job was to help his dad in the family shoe-repair business, and I only made $12.50 a week at my job at Park-Davis. I found out that he wouldn't look at me at church because he found me attractive and didn't want to even think about having a girl-friend when he didn't have a better job.

We were married just two months later, on February 15, 1934, at a Romanian church in Highland Park.

Raleigh's uncle, a man who had thirteen children himself and still managed to put on a buffet luncheon wedding for us at his home—said, "I don't have much to give you, but I'll give you a scripture verse from the Bible: 'Seek ye first the Kingdom of God and His righteousness and all these things will be added unto you.' If you live by it, the Lord will give you all that you have need of, pots, pans, linens, etc."

This word of prophecy was the best gift he could have given. Truly, the Lord *has* provided all we had need of over the past sixty-six years.

The Lord knew we needed a family; He provided it. Seven children, grandchildren, and great-grandchildren are a legacy and reward for following Him in ministry over the years. We attended the same church for over sixty-two years. All our kids were baptized in the same church; all were married in the same church; all graduated from the same grade school and the same high school.

The Heavenly Father entrusted me with sharing his Word to churches in Detroit and Windsor, Ontario, teaching at various levels with over thirty years, teaching youth how to understand God. I was honored to minister on a Windsor, Canada, radio station in the Romanian language on Sunday mornings for several years. I was able to serve in our children's school as kitchen chairman and later as president of the PTA for several years. The Lord opened opportunity for me to share the need to open all meetings with prayer and times to share His Word and direction for the elementary school and its parents. The mayor's wife became one of my best friends, and she opened doors with the state mental health director to speak at several of our PTA sessions. God is good, and His mercy endures forever.

We never had a fancy home, but it was always full of love, family, and friends. Our kids have often said how blessed they were that how they were taught to share and serve others. The Lord gave me wisdom on how to prepare meager but wholesome meals. Early days found Raleigh and me doing catering for large church parties, dinners, and weddings.

We felt it was important to have our doors open to our kids' friends and youth from the church. Often our kids would come after youth meetings and would ask me to put on a large pot of coffee. They would have twenty to thirty friends and a whole bunch of doughnuts or fresh bread and cold cuts. They'd have glorious times of fellowship, singing around the piano until 1:00 or 2:00 a.m.

We've been members of Bethesda Missionary Temple in Detroit (later moved to Sterling Heights). Raleigh worked as church custodian and head of maintenance for over thirty-two years until his retirement.

Back in my days, traveling with the mayor's wife, my kids would call me "our lady queen of the road." Now, as they push me in my wheelchair, I'm known as "queen of the wheels."

My Raleigh is witty, funny, smart, serious, honest, and a man of many words. He is known for his quotable quotes, like,

"God will supply *all* your *needs,* but you have to work hard for your wants."

Many looked at us as having such strong love that we never had disappointments or had any type of issues which created opposing positions, but that would be wrong. I will say this, because we were totally committed to God and each other, we endured where others would have failed. I found this note from my beloved that I forgot I had saved:

Forgive Me

Please Forgive Me
I Didn't Want to Make You Cry
Forgive Me, I Don't Want You to Sigh.
I Love You
And I Need You
We All Make Mistakes
Now & Then
I Love You My Dear,
And, Lets Be
Sweethearts Again.
To Dena, From Raleigh

Our life together was full of love and blessings that only God could provide, and I'm so glad I married the "man who wouldn't look up."

Slow Me Down, Lord

Ease the pounding of my heart by the quieting of my mind. Steady my hurried pace. Give me, amidst the day's confusion, the calmness of the everlasting hills.

Break the tensions of my nerves and muscles with the soothing music of singing streams that live in my memory.

Help me to know the magical, restoring power of sleep. Teach me the art of taking "minute vacations"…slowing down to look at a flower, to chat with a friend, to read a few lines from a good book.

Remind me of the fable of the hare and the tortoise; that the race is not always to the swift; that there is more to life than measuring its speed.

Let me look up at the branches of the towering oak and know that it grew slowly and well. Inspire me to send my own roots down deep into the soil of life's endearing values…that I may grow toward the stars of my greater destiny.

Slow me down, Lord.

(Wilferd Arlan Peterson, August 21, 1900–
June 2, 1995)

I posted a framed copy of this poem next to the back door to our home on Runyon. It was hanging on my janitor's room door at the church for more years than I can remember, and I really can't recall where I got it, but it seemed so fitting for a such an active life. The paper was tattered, and the frame was well worn, but the message rings true. One day my son Jim read it as I bustled past on one of my chores, and he asked me, pointedly, "Dad, have you I ever really read this?" I know he was probably trying to slow my retired pace down a bit. As I zoomed past it, I said with a smile, "I've never had time." It was a bit of a fib, but I'm sure God will forgive me; He always does.

Among My Senior Years

(To the tune of "Among My Souvenirs")
New Lyrics by Aurel Dikin Sr.

You think I don't know
That I am moving slow,
But when I have to go
I move much faster.

The steak I cannot eat
Because of store-bought teeth,
I live in misery
Among My Senior Years.

I once had thick dark hair
But now there's not much there,
Locks of Love I'd gladly share
God knows it isn't fair.

Although I love hard cheese
It always makes me sneeze,
And as I sadly wheeze
I think of yesterday.

My life has changed a lot
And, now I've finally got,
The time to share this spot
Among My Senior Years.

There's much more to life
Then woes and daily strife,
Thank God you've got a wife
Among these Senior Years

My hearing's almost gone
I had to buy some aid,
Now that the bill is paid
That gives me consolation.

I view the lovely birds
And, since I'm out of words,
I wish you all the best
Among *Your Senior Years*.